Organisational Culture for Information Managers

T0348779

CHANDOS
INFORMATION PROFESSIONAL SERIES

Series Editor: Ruth Rikowski
(email: Rikowskigr@aol.com)

Chandos' new series of books are aimed at the busy information professional. They have been specially commissioned to provide the reader with an authoritative view of current thinking. They are designed to provide easy-to-read and (most importantly) practical coverage of topics that are of interest to librarians and other information professionals. If you would like a full listing of current and forthcoming titles, please visit our web site www.chandospublishing.com or email info@chandospublishing.com or telephone +44 (0) 1223 499140.

New authors: we are always pleased to receive ideas for new titles; if you would like to write a book for Chandos, please contact Dr Glyn Jones on email gjones@chandospublishing.com or telephone number +44 (0) 1993 848726.

Bulk orders: some organisations buy a number of copies of our books. If you are interested in doing this, we would be pleased to discuss a discount. Please contact on email info@chandospublishing.com or telephone +44 (0) 1223 499140.

Organisational Culture for Information Managers

GILLIAN OLIVER

CP
CHANDOS
PUBLISHING

Oxford Cambridge New Delhi

Chandos Publishing
TBAC Business Centre
Avenue 4
Station Lane
Witney
Oxford OX28 4BN
UK
Tel: +44 (0) 1993 848726
Email: info@chandospublishing.com
www.chandospublishing.com

Chandos Publishing is an imprint of Woodhead Publishing Limited

Woodhead Publishing Limited
80 High Street
Sawston
Cambridge CB22 3HJ
UK
Tel: +44 (0) 1223 499140
Fax: +44 (0) 1223 832819
www.woodheadpublishing.com

First published in 2011

ISBN:
978 1 84334 650 0

© G. Oliver, 2011

Typeset by RefineCatch Limited, Bungay, Suffolk
Printed in the UK and USA.

Contents

List of tables

About the author

Gillian Oliver's background in information management spans libraries and records services in a number of diverse organisational settings. She is originally from London, where she completed her initial library studies qualification. She lived in Germany for ten years, and was Medical Library Consultant to hospitals run by the United States military in Europe.

Since moving to New Zealand her focus has changed to records and archives. After consulting for a wide range of public and private sector organisations, she developed a records and information management qualification for delivery by distance education. These experiences in very different cultural environments led to her doctoral research at Monash University, Melbourne, Australia, which investigated information cultures in three universities in different parts of the world. Gillian is currently Senior Lecturer in Archives and Records Management at Victoria University of Wellington, Wellington, New Zealand.

The author may be contacted at:

E-mail: *Gillian.Oliver@vuw.ac.nz*

Introduction

Abstract: This introduction to *Organisational Culture for Information Managers* provides the key information relating to the intent and purpose of the book. The scope of the book is organisational culture for information managers of all types, including both librarians and recordkeepers (records managers and archivists). Content of the book includes discussion of the concept itself and constituent layers (national, occupational and corporate culture), culminating in the introduction of the concept of information culture. Examples are provided of the practical implementation of projects tailored to suit different organisational settings.

Key words: organisational culture.

Scope and audience

The purpose of this book is to explain and explore the concept of organisational culture, specifically within the domain of information management. Understanding organisational culture is fundamentally important for anyone working in information management. In today's digital environment the workplace is characterised by individuals creating information often independently of formal systems, or even establishing new systems without cognisance of information management requirements. Consequently, no matter how technically correct your approaches are to managing information, whether you are working in a library, records services or archives setting, if you do not take into account the organisational culture success will be patchy at best. So the overriding purpose of this book is to emphasise the significance of organisational culture, and to explain the complexity and influence of this construct.

Often 'information management' is defined solely from the perspective of one occupational group, and understandably so. However, it is important to stress in this book that the perspectives of groups sometimes perceived to have competing interests are taken into account. The intended audience for this book is practitioners working in all occupations that make up the information management landscape, but primarily librarians, records managers and archivists. In addition, those currently studying for qualifications in these particular occupational groups should also find much of interest and value. In order to clearly distinguish those groups, the terminology used reflects Information Continuum[1] thinking. Information will often be referred to with reference to the primary purpose for which it is managed. So, information that is the focus of activities for records managers and archivists is referred to as 'information as evidence', managed for accountability purposes. The primary purpose of librarians is to manage information for knowledge or awareness, or for entertainment.

Structure

The book consists of seven chapters. Chapter 1 discusses the overall concept of organisational culture. It introduces the model which guides our exploration of culture in organisations, which is a multilayer one acknowledging the context in which the organisation exists. It explains why understanding organisational culture is so important for information managers and presents the ideas of the leading thinkers in this field. Particular attention is paid to the organisational culture theory of the Dutch anthropologist Geert Hofstede, as this is referred to throughout.

Chapter 2 focuses on the first and most fundamental layer in our cultural model: national culture. Again, the theory that is covered in most detail is that of Hofstede, and the characteristic dimensions identified by him are assessed in terms of their implications for information management. The following chapter departs from our layered organisational model by identifying structural features that influence organisational cultures. These structural features include language (considerations relating to the use of different character sets, and multiple languages), regional technological capabilities and the regulatory environment (particularly focusing on the laws which are so crucial to information management such as privacy, copyright and freedom of information). Legislation is culturally relevant from two perspectives: first in terms of its manifestation at a jurisdictional (national or regional, for instance) level and secondly in terms of employee awareness and acceptance of its provisions. These areas will greatly influence what happens as regards information management in organisations.

Chapters 4 and 5 each consider the two remaining layers of our organisational culture model: occupational and corporate culture. Occupational culture refers to the characteristics associated with the occupations or professions that people belong to. These characteristics can be very influential in terms of the way that people interact with information. This chapter also consider the occupational culture of information managers. Corporate culture refers to the uppermost and most superficial layer of organisational culture, the part that is the most susceptible to change.

The purpose of the final two chapters is to link all this theory clearly to the practice of information management. Chapter 6 focuses on information culture – the manifestations of organisational culture that portray values and attitudes to information in organisations. It describes a three-level framework to use for assessment of an organisation's information culture, and includes suggestions for how to find the relevant data for diagnosis. Finally, Chapter 7 presents a series of scenarios. These include establishing a special library service, developing a business case for a digital library, implementing an electronic document and records management system, and establishing an in-house archival repository. Each of these scenarios suggests strategies to take into account different organisational/information cultures.

Throughout the book, examples from my experience studying different organisational concepts are provided to illustrate the concepts under discussion. In addition to examples drawn from my normal working environment in New Zealand, others are taken from a series of case studies, which compared information management at three universities, each situated in places where there were likely to be cultural differences (Australia, Hong Kong and Germany). In addition, further examples are used from a period spent at Tallinn University, Estonia. Most chapters conclude with suggestions for further reading.

Understanding organisational culture and using that understanding to develop tailored strategies for information management is a demanding undertaking requiring that information managers accept that there is no one-size-fits-all approach. However, the benefits in terms of successful organisational information management that are likely to accrue will be substantial.

Note

1. Teaching tool developed by Barbara Reed, Don Schauder and Frank Upward of the School of Information Management & Systems, Monash University.

1

The significance of organisational culture

Abstract: This chapter explains the concept of organisational culture and establishes why it is necessary for information managers to understand this. The values accorded to information and attitudes to it are indicative of the information culture of organisations; understanding organisational culture will enable the development of appropriate strategies and systems. Two contrasting views of organisational culture are discussed, one which assumes culture is solely internally based and the other which acknowledges the external environment in which the organisation is situated.

Key words: organisational culture, information culture, national culture.

Introduction

This chapter begins by discussing why it is important to understand organisational culture. Then I start to establish what organisational culture encompasses. Although it is a term that most people are familiar with, and many use frequently when discussing their workplace, interpretation and understanding vary greatly. Two of the key perspectives are discussed, one of which has unfortunately been very prevalent and influential on management thinking, to the detriment of information management. The final section of this chapter outlines the multilevel approach to organisational culture that underpins the thinking in this book, acknowledging the existence of national, occupational and corporate cultural influences in shaping our working environments.

Why is understanding organisational culture so important?

Whether you are a librarian, records manager or archivist, the objective of your work is to manage information. The primary purpose for which you are attempting to manage information will vary according to your occupation. Records managers and archivists manage information as evidence, for accountability. Librarians manage information for knowledge and awareness, and also sometimes for entertainment. So far, so good. These distinct purposes provide a universality for the work undertaken by information managers and enable us to work collaboratively (regionally, nationally and globally) to explore and develop appropriate technologies, systems and processes. However, the specific organisational context that librarians, records managers and archivists are working within is a primary influence on the way that they go about achieving their work objectives. For example, the way in which you would go about ensuring your clients are mindful of their information management obligations in a very structured setting such as a law firm would be quite different to a more anarchic environment such as a university.

Most information managers fulfil key roles in providing the necessary infrastructure to enable the organisation that they serve to function efficiently and effectively. But the nature of that organisation will vary widely, according to a number of factors, in particular

- *Geography* – Where the organisation is situated, whether it is multinational or restricted to one region or country. These features will determine the legislative environment, the languages used by employees and customers, and national cultural characteristics. Also of critical importance are the information and communication technology (ICT) capabilities of the location. For example, ready access to wireless internet facilities will be a significant influencer on the expectations of employees for accessing and creating information.

- *The functions of the organisation* – These will determine the legislation and standards that the organisation is subject to, which in turn will influence the types of information created and required to be accessed and retained.

- *The management of the organisation* – This may affect the priority accorded to managing information, and resourcing of those activities. Also, the priorities accorded to information systems, information literacy and digital literacy skills of staff throughout the organisation will in turn impact on the success of information management initiatives.

These factors are intertwined, and are likely to influence each other, but all play a role in shaping the culture of the organisation. Each of these will be explored further in this book.

Understanding the importance of these factors will enable the diagnosis of an organisation's information culture – that is, the values accorded to information, and attitudes towards it, specifically within organisational contexts. Every organisation, no matter how large or small, regardless of type and function, wherever in the world it is situated, has an information culture. Table 1.1 presents a framework for the assessment of information culture; the levels are explored in Chapter 6.

Table 1.1	Framework for information culture assessment
Level One	*The base or fundamental layer can be assessed by consideration of:* ■ **Respect for information as evidence.** Recognition and awareness of the need to manage certain information for the purposes of accountability. ■ **Respect for information as knowledge.** Recognition and awareness of the need to manage certain information for the purpose of increasing knowledge and awareness. ■ **Willingness to share information.** The level of granularity to which information sharing is regarded as the norm within the organisation. ■ **Trust in information.** This will focus on consideration of preferred primary sources for information, for example, individuals or text resources. ■ **Language requirements.** There may be constraints associated with particular character sets used and also the need for multilingual versions of information. ■ **Regional technological infrastructure.** The technological infrastructure in place externally will be a profound influencing factor on the dimensions of the information culture within an organisation.
Level Two	*Skills, knowledge and experience related to information management, which can be acquired and/or extended in the workplace:* ■ Information-related competencies, including information and computer literacy. ■ Awareness of environmental (societal and organisational) requirements relating to information.
Level Three	*The third and uppermost layer is reflected in:* ■ The information governance model that is in place. ■ Trust in organisational systems.

Information culture is inextricably intertwined with organisational culture, and it is only by understanding the organisation that progress can be made with information management initiatives.

Organisations are microcosms of their broader societal context. They may appear to be self-contained, but definitely do not exist in isolation from their broader context. Often consideration of organisational culture focuses solely on internal factors, primarily management and resourcing. The key aim of this book, however, is to highlight and untangle all those features that influence what happens at the library, records service or archives.

One of the features that characterise information management is the sheer diversity of settings in which it is implemented. For that reason, many practitioners remain in the same environment and it can be difficult to swap settings, largely because of the specialist skills and knowledge required. A law librarian, for instance, attempting to change focus to a hospital setting will often be regarded as making a career shift and may find entry into the new field problematic. Consequently, any consideration given to the more fine-grained or nuanced aspects of organisational culture is often overlooked. Where there is differentiation according to setting in literature and guidelines for practice, this is generally restricted to broad-brush domains such as medicine and law. Nevertheless, the work of information managers in, say, hospitals in various parts of the world, although focused on the same outcomes, may be quite different in terms of priorities accorded to different services and activities.

The ways in which information managers will be affected by organisational culture will vary according to the extent to which the main elements of their work (users and materials) are internal to the organisation, or external. For example:

■ Special librarians in businesses, government departments, hospitals and so on will customise services to suit the needs of their clientele, who are likely to be generally internal to the organisation. Those needs will reflect, and be influenced by, the culture of the organisation.

■ Records managers and archivists in similar settings also have the challenge of customising and targeting services.

In addition, the environment will greatly impact on the information itself that is the focus of their information management goals, namely, the ways in which records are created, managed and stored by individuals.

- In public library settings, organisational cultural challenges will be experienced not so much from the user or information perspective, but in dealing with the parent body. Public librarians have to understand the organisational culture of the local authority in which they are operating, in order to formulate appropriate strategies and present them in such a way as to facilitate acceptance.

- In further educational settings such as universities, clients will vary much more widely on the spectrum of internal to external. Students occupy more ambiguous territory as they are officially part of the organisation, but may be quite peripheral, especially if study is on a part-time basis. Also the complexity of the subcultures associated with the different disciplines that make up the university is enormously challenging.

Organisational culture and information management – academic research

There is an extensive body of literature published about research into information technologies and culture, including organisational and national comparative studies. The growth of multinational organisations, and deployment of information and communication technologies facilitating the globalisation of business have brought cross-cultural management and communication issues to the fore. An analysis of articles published in the leading information systems journals over a nine-year period identified over three hundred articles relating to global information management, i.e. 'the development, use and management of information systems in a global/international context' (Gallupe & Tan, 1999: 1).

In contrast to information systems, there has been very little published research on the role of organisational and/ or national culture in the library and recordkeeping fields. J. Periam Danton proposed an outline curriculum for the study of comparative librarianship and suggested a methodology to investigate this area (Danton, 1973). More recently, library researchers have been encouraged to include cross-cultural comparisons, and useful areas for study have been identified as intellectual policy legislation, regulation of mass media, science policy, censorship and library services, rather than the 'tourist-type' descriptive report which is commonly found in library and information studies journals (Buckland & Gathegi, 1991). Philip Calvert (2001) used Hofstede's dimensions to assess whether attitudes to service quality in academic library users were influenced by national culture. He notes that despite its suitability for this kind of study, Hofstede's work does not appear to have been used before in information and library studies research (Calvert, 2001). Carolyn McSwiney discusses Hofstede's dimensions in terms of information-seeking behaviour, and makes recommendations for librarians working in a multicultural context (McSwiney, 2003). Jennifer Rowley includes a brief discussion of the need to take into account national differences when determining knowledge management strategy, and proposing technological solutions (Rowley, 2003), and library practitioners are encouraged to take corporate culture into account when assessing library services (see Budd, 1996 for instance).

There are anecdotal accounts of national differences in recordkeeping practice, in the same vein as the 'tourist-type' literature mentioned by Buckland and Gathegi (1991).

However, there has also been consideration of cultural interactions and influences at a more scholarly level. David Bearman contrasts approaches in the United States and Europe to the management of electronic records, which he attributes to different cultural contexts, and suggests connections between Hofstede's dimensions and archival practice (Bearman, 1992). Eric Ketelaar has drawn attention to national differences in archival systems, strategies and methodologies and in doing so advocated a comparative archival science to explore these differences (Ketelaar, 1997b, 1999, 2001, 2005).

The Electronic Recordkeeping Research project of the University of Pittsburgh developed a model for developing functional requirements for electronic records based on warrant. Warrant is defined as the 'mandate from law, professional best practices, and other social sources requiring the creation and continued maintenance of records' (Cox & Duff, 1997: 223). It is suggested that warrant is the most important aspect of the Pittsburgh project calling for additional study. The culture of the organisation can be considered as an aspect of warrant, including the industry in which the organisation is based and country in which the organisation is situated. Elizabeth Yakel (1996) also discusses the importance of organisational culture in recordkeeping and considers Duranti's work on diplomatics in the cultural context.

Research into ethical issues which will have an effect on the management of information in organisations has been reported within information systems, management and accountancy literature. For example, the effect of national culture on audit practice has been investigated. Tsui and Windsor (2001) compared ethical reasoning in auditors from China and Australia, and the results were consistent with Hofstede's predictions. Cohen and colleagues (1993) consider possible ethical conflicts for a multinational accounting practice in the context of Hofstede's dimensions. Ethical attitudes involved in day-to-day decision making by managers have been investigated in a multinational study, differences were found in countries with differing values for Hofstede's individualism-collectivism and uncertainty avoidance dimensions (Jackson, 2001).

Global information systems, e-commerce initiatives and the existence of multinational enterprises have highlighted differing attitudes and regulatory systems with regard to the protection of personal information. Sandra Milberg and colleagues (1995) conducted research to investigate firstly relationships between nationality, cultural values and privacy concerns, and secondly whether cultural values and privacy concerns are associated with different policy approaches. In doing so they used a continuum model to illustrate the global variation in regulatory approaches – ranging from non-governmental intervention to high governmental involvement. Results from their research indicate that the extent of government involvement is affected by cultural values (p. 71). A relationship between national culture, privacy policy and practice has been confirmed by a number of authors (Ajami, 1990; Cockcroft, 2002; Cockcroft & Clutterbuck, 2001; Duff et al., 2001).

Trans-border data flow legislation (TDFL) is a specific manifestation of privacy concerns. TDFL is designed to check the free flow of certain types of information (including personal information) across national boundaries. Walczuch et al. (1995) state that the main motivation for TDFL is cultural, although there may be other contributing factors. They analyse existing policy and regulatory environments, and relate this analysis to Hofstede's dimensions. They conclude that the power distance and individualism dimensions appear to correlate with the adoption of TDFL (p. 54).

Walczuch and Steeghs (2001) consider the European Union (EU) directive on data protection legislation in depth and state that is a 'typically European phenomenon' (p. 143). However, they emphasise that there are major cultural differences between European nations.

My own research has explored similarities and differences in information management practices between organisations situated in different parts of the world. One study compared three universities situated in Australia, Germany and Hong Kong respectively. Although the functions of these organisations were the same (all were specialist distance education providers) information management in each had quite different features. The main characteristics of each were as follows.

In the Australian university:

- Management of information was not holistic, it was fragmented across the organisation.
- There was little awareness on the part of individuals of records management responsibilities, and employees showed little trust in the records management systems that were in place.
- People complained about information silos.
- A technological solution was proposed as the means of fixing all information management problems.
- People were generally positive about sharing information with colleagues.
- There was a disjuncture between society's and the university's framework for information management – i.e. a mismatch between external standards and policy.
- People seemed more inclined to ask a colleague for information rather than consult a documentary resource.

In the German university:

- A holistic approach was taken to the management of information, taking into account the needs of all stakeholders, including both staff and students.
- Efficient and effective systems were in place to share and disseminate information.
- A high value was accorded to information of all types.
- High importance was accorded to textual information – regarded as authentic and trustworthy.
- Explicit links were made between societal requirements and internal policies, i.e. reference made to specific legislative requirements in policy documents.
- There were no complaints or comments about information silos.
- Staff showed a strong sense of the need to show accountability by keeping records.

In the Hong Kong university:

- Records management was not viewed as a necessary function.
- There were concerns about the consequences of archiving information because of the perceived risk of unauthorised access to it.
- Staff showed reluctance to share information with colleagues beyond their immediate workgroup.
- There was minimal policy or systems relating to information management, which reflected the societal framework.
- Shortcomings in information technology systems were addressed by using support staff to manually process information.

Differences then between the universities were reflected in the:

- organisational models (respectively the market, well-oiled machine and family model discussed in Chapter 2);
- attitudes to sharing information;
- preferences for textual or oral information;
- the value and recognition accorded to records (information as evidence);
- the ways in which technology was used to manage information;
- the information governance models in place (see further discussion in Chapter 6).

As this was interpretive research, findings cannot be generalised across whole countries. However, this study did highlight areas where organisational culture may influence information management.

In summary, looking at the academic literature it can be seen that although comparatively little research has been undertaken investigating culture in library and recordkeeping disciplines, there is much that is relevant to these areas (such as attitudes to privacy and ethical considerations) in other disciplines.

What is organisational culture?

Before going any further it is important to be very clear about the meaning and nature of organisational culture. Culture is a concept that is the focal point of studies in many different disciplines including anthropology, sociology and psychology. Within information management, culture can be regarded as primarily of interest because of the artefacts that are products of particular cultures, and so is often referred to from a heritage viewpoint. The organisations in which many information managers work may be referred to as 'cultural heritage' institutions. Establishing a clear definition of culture that is appropriate to all disciplines and all perspectives is extremely unlikely, and probably attempting to do this undesirable. Therefore I will focus on just one interpretation, which regards culture from a perspective of shared values.

The definition of culture used in this book is that of psychology professor Harry Triandis (1972: 4) of the University of Illinois, who defined culture as a 'group's characteristic way of perceiving the man-made part of its environment'. He suggests that this perception is likely to be shared by 'people who live next to one another, speak the same dialect, and engage in similar activities (e.g. have similar occupations)' (p. 4). The wording used in this definition acknowledges the possibility of difference between individuals, and does not imply that values are fixed and immutable. This definition is preferred because it emphasises the fact that culture should not only be considered from a geographical perspective, but there are in fact various facets or layers of culture which will be influential. The concept of various layers of culture is further discussed below.

'Organisational culture' is a phrase widely and loosely used. The connotations of the phrase are often taken to refer to cultural characteristics that are unique to a particular organisation. People may talk about on the one hand having a 'good organisational culture' or even a 'regular' organisational culture, and on the other hand a 'dysfunctional' or 'problem' organisational culture.

This limited view of organisational culture can be traced to the management literature, in particular Tom Peters and Robert Waterman's 1982 highly influential book *In Search of Excellence: Lessons from America's best-run companies*. These authors attributed organisational excellence to the existence of a 'strong' culture:

> Without exception, the dominance and coherence of culture proved to be an essential quality of the excellent companies. Moreover, the stronger the culture and the more it was directed toward the marketplace, the less need was there for policy manuals, organisation charts, or detailed procedures and roles. (p. 75)

Peters and Waterman identified the following factors as the eight attributes of excellence:

1. A bias for action.
2. Closeness to the customer.
3. Autonomy and entrepreneurship.
4. Productivity through people.
5. Hands-on, value driven.
6. Stick to the knitting.
7. Simple form, lean staff.
8. Simultaneous loose-tight properties.

In Search of Excellence makes very interesting reading from an information management perspective, not only because it has been influential in creating a partial or misleading view of organisational culture. More significantly, there is much that is explicitly associated with the Peters and Waterman definition of 'good' organisational cultures that can be actually detrimental to information management. Written information (such as the detailed procedures and policy manuals mentioned above) is depicted as being a sign of an inadequate culture, so it is likely that records management functions would not be highly valued. With regard to the eight attributes, the last two in particular can actually be seen as negative influences on establishing and maintaining information management services. With respect to the seventh attribute, Peters and Waterman state that: 'Top-level staffs are lean; it is not uncommon to find a corporate staff of fewer than 100 people running multi-billion-dollar enterprises' (p. 15).

Information management functions are often part of the central corporate services allocation, so any aspirations for leanness will almost inevitably lead to questioning of the value of associated positions. Unless the organisation concerned has a champion in senior management that will protect and promote information management, this can be a serious risk to survival for information management services.

Similarly, the final attribute signifies that chaos is acceptable, implying that little importance should be placed on establishing or requiring adherence to organisational systems. This type of environment would not be optimal for successful information management, especially the systematic creation and management of records for accountability.

Needless to say, this view of organisational culture is not one that is adopted in this book. Describing organisational cultures as strong or weak has very little meaning. As we will see, what appears 'good' in one setting may very well be regarded as completely dysfunctional in another. Nevertheless, it is very important to be aware of this perspective of organisational culture, and indeed the negative effect it can have on information management activities. In discussing organisational cultural issues with management or colleagues, it is worth spending some time making sure that you are not talking at cross purposes. Like it or not, the Peters and Waterman view of organisational culture has certainly made its mark, and it is important to understand it in order to be able to present an alternative, more rounded view.

Moving to the much more holistic approach to organisational culture that we adopt in this book, one very influential scholar who has explored the underlying concepts is Edgar Schein, professor of management at the Massachusetts Institute of Technology. He distinguishes three levels at which cultural analysis can take place: artefacts, beliefs and values, and finally underlying assumptions (Schein, 2004: 25–37). These levels are further described as follows:

- *Artefacts*. A very comprehensive term, denoting all the very diverse phenomena that are readily visible. So, this will include for instance the architecture and interior design of the organisation, its language and ways of communicating, its technologies, the stories that circulate about past and present employees and leaders. Schein also classifies the more formal aspects of the workplace as artefacts – such as processes, procedures and organisational charts.

- *Beliefs and values*. Schein identifies these as strategies, goals and philosophies. He stresses the importance of the beliefs and values that are promulgated in the organisation to be based on prior learning on the part of employees. If this is not the case, the beliefs and values may only influence what is *said* in a given situation, rather than what is actually *done*.

- *Underlying assumptions*. These are the taken-for-granted norms that people may have very little awareness of simply because they are so fundamental to the way that things are done. Consequently they can be extremely difficult to change. To illustrate, Schein refers to an engineer deliberately designing a product as unsafe as an inconceivable example of a flawed underlying assumption.

I will refer back to artefacts in particular later in Chapter 5, but the model that we will use for organisational culture as a concept is one that explicitly takes into account the external setting of the organisation. The approach is that organisational culture is a comprehensive term, which encompasses features that reflect the geographical situation of the organisation, the occupations of the people that work within it, as well as any other cultural characteristics that are unique to that specific institution.

This book will focus on organisational culture in its widest possible sense, that is including the main cultural influences which will impact in one way or another on work within an organisation. This acknowledges that the values and beliefs of individuals will not be solely created or even shaped by the organisation in which they work. This is acknowledged in Schein's 'underlying assumptions', and explicitly linked to national culture by the Dutch anthropologist Geert Hofstede. Hofstede is best known for developing a model for the measurement of national cultural dimensions, which we will consider in some detail in Chapter 2. Hofstede's theory relating to national culture is subject to considerable debate, which can detract from the insight that his work has contributed to understanding organisational culture. For this reason, it is worthwhile at this initial stage to present the main features relating to Hofstede's study, and in particular the main criticisms, as a prelude to introducing his organisational culture theory which underpins the thinking in this book.

In the latter part of the twentieth century, surveys were conducted to measure the attitudes of employees of IBM in over 70 countries. The analysis of the data that was collected from these surveys formed the basis of Hofstede's theory relating to the fundamental influences on our behaviour. Hofstede has described these influences as 'software of the mind' and provides the following explanation of his thinking:

> . . . people carry 'mental programs' that are developed in the family in early childhood and reinforced in

> schools and organisations, and … these mental programs contain a component of national culture. They are most clearly expressed in the different values that predominate among people from different countries. (Hofstede, 2001, p. xix)

Hofstede's research has been the subject of criticism and debate, as well as replication and application. Other models of national culture will be described in Chapter 2, but Hofstede's is by far the most extensively cited in academic literature (a search on Google Scholar indicates tens of thousands of cited references to Hofstede's work). The main areas of criticism of Hofstede's theory are that:

- The cultural dimensions are reflective of the world as it was in the 1970s, and consequently are no longer relevant to today's environment.
- The survey population of IBM, being largely white collar, middle class employees, cannot be considered as representative of entire nations.
- A questionnaire on its own was insufficient to gather information relating to values (Sondergaard, 1994).

The first two criticisms can be countered with reference to the considerable number of surveys in wide-ranging settings that have been conducted subsequently, using Hofstede's methodology. For example, a much more recent large-scale study which included 43 countries indicated considerable replicability from the previous value surveys covering large numbers of countries (Smith et al., 1996).

The final criticism relating to reliance on a questionnaire rather than more in-depth interviews to gather data is recognised by Hofstede himself and he recognises the need for, and encourages, other approaches:

> The ideal study of culture would combine idiographic
> and nomothetic, emic and etic, qualitative and
> quantitative elements . . . The nomothetic approach in
> the present study is a consequence of the type of data
> that became available . . . The idiographic element in
> my research is that I had frequently visited and interacted
> intensively with a fair number of the participating
> national IBM subsidiaries during the organisation of
> the first survey cycle. My interpretations of the scores
> found are often based on personal observations and
> profound discussions with locals of different ranks . . .
> I admire other, more idiographic and qualitative
> approaches. (Hofstede, 2001: 26)

There is also a more fundamental criticism of Hofstede's
work that applies to all national cultural models: these
research findings over-simplify culture by equating it with
nations.

There are indeed obvious limitations when defining culture
by equating it with a nation. Nations are not fixed and
immutable; political changes, particularly in Europe, have
demonstrated that to us all too clearly. A political entity
identified as a nation or country is likely to be made up of a
number of distinct ethnic groups which may be characterised
by different value sets. It must therefore be emphasised that
at the organisational level, it is recognised that employees
will of course hold values representative of particular ethnic,
religious and linguistic groupings within that nation. Hofstede
clearly acknowledges the existence of such subcultures.

Finally it must be noted that Hofstede's theory does not
apply to individuals per se, but rather reflects the tendency or
likelihood to hold certain values. It is important to remember
the meaning of Hofstede's model, and guard against making
the erroneous assumptions that:

- All members of a culture homogeneously carry the same cultural attributes, that a culture can be uniform.

- Values and behaviour of all individuals will be wholly determined by their cultural background.

- Dimensions are direct measures of national culture – they are not, they are manifestations of national culture (Williamson, 2002).

The model of culture referred to by Geert Hofstede and colleagues in a 1990 study is the one that underpins the approach to organisational culture in this book. Similar to Schein's approach, these authors describe a multilevel model, identifying three layers of culture which are influential in organisations (Hofstede et al., 1990).

The initial layer I will refer to for the sake of simplicity as national culture, where the values acquired growing up from family and school influence attitudes and activities. The middle layer is occupational culture – those values and practices which have been learned in the course of vocational education and training. The most superficial layer reflects those characteristics that are unique to the organisation, the corporate culture. The sector or industry that the organisation is engaged in will be significant, as will the occupational groupings working inside the organisation. Each of these layers will be considered in detail in the rest of the book.

Hofstede (2001: 11) portrays the manifestations of culture as layers around a core of values. Detmar Straub and co-authors (2002) take this a step further and use an analogy of a virtual onion, where the layers are permeable and do not have a given order or sequence, to convey the complexity and lack of predictability of an individual's cultural characteristics (p. 14). There has been very little research into the relative influences of these cultural layers. What must be emphasised at the outset, therefore, is that the degree of prevalence of one layer over another is not pre-determined. Depending on the setting, the relative influences of the various layers will vary greatly.

Summary and conclusions

Organisational culture has a profound influence on the way in which information is managed. Values and attitudes to information within organisations reflect its information culture; assessment of the information culture is dependent upon understanding the organisational culture.

The concept of organisational culture is widely referred to and discussed, but understanding and interpretation varies enormously. The definition frequently found in management literature of a strong or good organisational culture is not helpful and may even be detrimental to successful information management. The approach taken to organisational culture in this book follows that of Hofstede in distinguishing three levels of cultural characteristics which will shape the overall organisational culture: national, occupational and corporate culture. The relative importance of these three levels is not clear cut, and will vary according to the setting of the workplace. In the next chapter I will look in more detail at the first of these layers: national culture.

References

Ajami, R. (1990) Transborder data flow: global issues of concern, values and options. In S. B. Lundstedt (ed.), *Telecommunications, Values, and the Public Interest* (pp. 126–43). Norwood, NJ: Ablex.

Bearman, D. (1992) Diplomatics, Weberian bureaucracy, and the management of electronic records in Europe and America. *American Archivist, 55*(1), 168–81.

Buckland, M. K., & Gathegi, J. N. (1991) International aspects of LIS research. In C. R. McClure & P. Hernon (Eds.), *Library and Information Science Research: Perspectives and strategies for improvement* (pp. 63–71). Norwood, NJ: Ablex.

Budd, J. M. (1996) The organizational culture of the research university: Implications for LIS education. *Journal of Education for Library and Information Science, 37*(2), 154–62.

Calvert, P. J. (2001) International variations in measuring customer expectations. *Library Trends, 49*(4), 732–53.

Cockcroft, S. (2002) Gaps between policy and practice in the protection of data privacy. *Journal of Information Technology Theory and Application, 4*(3), 1–13.

Cockcroft, S., & Clutterbuck, P. (2001) *Attitudes towards information privacy.* Paper presented at the Proceedings of the 12th Australasian Conference on Information Systems, Coffs Harbour, NSW.

Cohen, J. R., Pant, L. W., & Sharp, D. J. (1993) Culture-based ethical conflicts confronting multinational accounting firms. *Accounting Horizons, 7*(3), 1–13.

Cox, R. J., & Duff, W. M. (1997) Warrant and the definition of electronic records: questions arising from the Pittsburgh Project. *Archives and Museum Informatics, 11*(3/4), 223–31.

Danton, J. P. (1973) *The Dimensions of Comparative Librarianship.* Chicago: American Library Association.

Duff, W. M., Smielauskas, W., & Yoos, H. (2001) Protecting privacy. *Information Management Journal, 35*(2), 14–30.

Gallupe, R. B., & Tan, F. (1999) A research manifesto for global information management. *Journal of Global Information Management*, 7(3), 5.

Hofstede, G. (2001) *Culture's Consequences: Comparing values, behaviors, institutions, and organizations across nations* (2nd edn.). Thousand Oaks, CA: Sage Publications.

Hofstede, G., Neuijen, B., Ohayv, D. D., & Sanders, G. (1990) Measuring organizational cultures: a qualitative and quantitative study across twenty cases. *Administrative Science Quarterly*, 35(2), 286–316.

Jackson, T. (2001) Cultural values and management ethics: A 10 nation study. *Human Relations*, 54(10), 1267–1302.

Ketelaar, E. (1997) The difference best postponed? *Archivaria*, 44, 142–48. *www.hum.uva.nl/bai/home/eketelaar/difference.doc*

Ketelaar, E. (1999) Archivalisation and archiving. *Archives and Manuscripts*, 27(1), 54–61.

Ketelaar, E. (2001) Ethnologie archivistique. *Gazette des Archives*, 192, 7–20.

Ketelaar, E. (2005) *'Control through communication' in a comparative perspective*. Paper presented at the Proceedings of the First International Conference on the History of Records and Archives (I-CHORA) (forthcoming).

McSwiney, C. (2003) Cultural implications of a global context: the need for the reference librarian to ask again 'who is my client?'. *Australian Library Journal*, 52(4), 379–88.

Milberg, S. J., Burke, S. J., Smith, J., & Kallman, E. A. (1995) Values, personal information privacy, and regulatory approaches. *Communications of the ACM*, 38(12), 65–74.

Peters, T. J. & Waterman, R. H. (1982) *In Search of Excellence: Lessons from America's best-run companies*. New York: Harper & Row.

Rowley, J. (2003) Knowledge management – the new librarianship? From custodians of history to gatekeepers to the future. *Library Management*, 24(8/9), 433–40.

Schein, E. H. (2004) *Organizational Culture and Leadership* (3rd edn.). San Francisco: Jossey-Bass.

Smith, P. B., Dugan, S., & Trompenaars, F. (1996) National culture and the values of organizational employees: A dimensional analysis across 43 nations. *Journal of Cross-Cultural Psychology*, 27(2), 231–64.

Sondergaard, M. (1994) Hofstede's consequences: A study of reviews, citations and replications. *Organization Studies*, 15(3), 447–56.

Straub, D., Loch, K., Evaristo, R., Karahanna, E., & Srite, M. (2002) Toward a theory-based measurement of culture. *Journal of Global Information Management*, 10(1), 13–24.

Triandis, H. C. (1972) *The Analysis of Subjective Culture*. New York: Wiley.

Tsui, J., & Windsor, C. (2001) Some cross-cultural evidence on ethical reasoning. *Journal of Business Ethics*, 31(2), 143–50.

Walczuch, R. M., Singh, S. K., & Palmer, T. S. (1995) An analysis of the cultural motivations for transborder data flow legislation. *Information Technology and People*, 8(2), 37–57.

Walczuch, R. M., & Steeghs, L. (2001) Implications of the new EU Directive on data protection for multinational corporations. *Information Technology and People*, 14(2), 142–62.

Williamson, D. (2002) Forward from a critique of Hofstede's model of national culture. *Human Relations*, 55(11), 1373–95.

Yakel, E. (1996) The way things work: Procedures, processes, and institutional records. *American Archivist*, 59, 454–64.

Further reading

Hofstede, G., Hofstede, G. J. & Minkov, M. (2010) *Cultures and Organizations: Software of the Mind* (3rd edn.). New York: McGraw Hill.

Oliver, G. (2008) Information culture: Exploration of differing values and attitudes to information in organisations. *Journal of Documentation*, 64(3), 363–85.

2

National culture

Abstract: This chapter considers national cultural characteristics. The problems inherent in defining national cultures are discussed, and the dangers of relying on stereotypes or caricatures are emphasised. The Hall contextual model is described, but most detail is reserved for the multidimensional model of national culture developed by Geert Hofstede. Each of the Hofstede dimensions is described and the implications for information management are discussed.

Key words: national culture, power distance, uncertainty avoidance, individualism, collectivism.

Introduction

In this chapter I will explore the underlying level of our organisational culture model, national culture, or the characteristics associated with 'the collective programming of the mind acquired by growing up in a particular country' (Hofstede, 1997: 262). First I will consider the controversy surrounding national culture as a construct, and then various interpretations or models will be described. The majority of this chapter is devoted to discussion of Hofstede's dimensions, and consideration of possible implications for information management.

The debate surrounding national culture

Any exploration of national culture has to be approached with caution. It is only too easy to fall into the trap of identifying stereotypes or caricatures. These national caricatures are simplistically drawn, therefore easily recognised and provide ready fodder for humour and populist politicians. Nationalities that are the target of jokes and more sinister attention vary according to geographical location and the presence or absence of societal forces, such as economic recession and immigration. So, it must be very strongly emphasised at the outset that the objective of our consideration of national culture is not to construct neat little stereotypes that can be applied to forecast the behaviour of individuals. My goal is to provide insight into the diversity of values and attitudes of people working in organisations towards information, and to show that there are multiple perspectives at play.

In the previous chapter I looked at the problems associated with equating culture with a particular country. To recap, I established unequivocally that there are major limitations to defining culture by equating it with a nation or country. What constitutes a nation, and the lack of permanence associated with nationhood are significant problem areas. The political boundaries of a nation are likely to contain distinct ethnic groups holding different cultural characteristics or values. This ethnic diversity is likely to be represented within organisations, adding a further element of complexity to the overall organisational culture. The objective in this chapter is to identify tendencies to hold certain values, rather than establishing hard and fast rules applicable to individuals.

Political and social changes which have contributed to increasing globalisation would seem to have emphasised cultural differences, rather than minimised them. As Frances Fukuyama states, 'one of the ironies of the convergence of larger institutions since the end of the cold war is that people around the world are now even more conscious of the cultural differences that separate them' (Fukuyama, 1995: 5).

Hence despite debates about the validity of national culture as a construct, interest in cultural differences seems to be increasing rather than diminishing. Organisations today are likely to conduct business internationally and multinational enterprises may face unexpected challenges in managing information. Different regulatory environments (for example, variations in copyright, privacy and freedom of information legislation) will pose one set of challenges, and these in turn will reflect possibly wide variation in attitudes and opinions relating to information. The regulatory environment will be discussed further in the next chapter.

Models of national culture

Given increasing globalisation, significant research effort has been directed towards developing models of national culture. We will consider the cultural dimensions associated with the Dutch anthropologist Hofstede's model in detail. But before doing so, it is worth noting other models of national culture that are sometimes referred to in the literature.

Frances Fukuyama, quoted above, developed a theory based on the analysis of a single variable, trust. He associates this with the notion of shared social capital, which he explains as follows:

> Social capital consists of norms or values, instantiated in an actual relationship among two or more people, that promote cooperation between them. These norms

and values can range from the relatively superficial, like friends who share a love of cooking or hiking, to highly complex, like the value systems underlying organised religion. (Fukuyama, 2001: 480)

Another relatively simple cultural model is that of respected American academic Edward T. Hall (Hall, 1976). The Hall model uses a single continuum of high to low context to plot cultural differences. Preferences for high or low context are of key concern in information management. Where high context communication is preferred, the emphasis is on the context rather than content. In other words, critical communication takes place based not just on what is explicitly stated, which can be the minor source of information with respect to contextual information inherent in the person and/or environment. Low context communication, however, necessitates that as much information as possible has to be made explicit for communication to be successful. So, pictures and images could be much more effective than text in situations where the preference is for high-context communication. This has particular implications for information management, and as high/low context are also features of Hofstede's model will be discussed later in this chapter under 'Individualism/Collectivism'.

Another feature identified in the Hall model is attitudes to time. The two extremes are monochronic (paying attention to one thing at a time) and polychronic (paying attention to many things at once). This is an interesting feature to consider, which may influence the choice of communication tools used in today's digital working environment. A combination of online text and oral communication may be more easily dealt with by polychronics (multi-taskers) than monochronics. Although there is much that is relevant to information managers in the Hall model, the main problem with it is that it has not been rigorously tested (Cardon, 2008).

There are two major multidimension models of culture with global applicability. Hofstede's model identifies five dimensions, and the other model developed by Charles Hampden-Turner and Frans Trompenaars distinguishes seven dimensions (Hampden-Turner & Trompenaars, 1994). Although the terminology used in the two models differs, the factors measured by both are very similar. The matrix shown in Table 2.1 was developed by researchers in the information systems domain, and demonstrates the commonality in the two models.

Table 2.1 Mapping of Trompenaars' and Hofstede's dimensions

Trompenaars' dimensions	Hofstede's dimensions			
	Power distance	Masculinity v. Feminity	Uncertainty avoidance	Individualism v. Collectivism
Universalism v. Particularism			X	
Neutral v. Emotional	X	X	X	
Individualism v. Collectivism				X
Specific v. Diffuse	X		X	
Achievement v. Ascription		X		
Attitudes to time		X	X	
Attitudes to the environment		X		

Source: Krumbholz and Maiden, 2001: 189.

Of these two models, Hofstede's has been the most frequently replicated, tested and validated, and is therefore the one used in this book. *Culture's Consequences* has been cited over 2,000 times according to the *Social Science Citation Index*, with most citations appearing in cross-cultural and organisational psychology, organisational sociology, management and communication (Hofstede, 2001: 462). A recent attempt to cross-validate Hofstede's classification is particularly interesting in that it explored the reflection of national culture by organisations (van Oudenhoven, 2001). This study found considerable correlation between Hofstede's dimensions and culture as perceived in organisations, but there was very little relationship between culture as perceived and culture as desired by respondents. My interpretation of this finding is that it demonstrates the fundamental nature of the dimensions of national culture. Any modifications or changes to those cultural values will be very slow and will not occur simply because management decides to 'change the culture'. In contrast, if changes occur to these values this will take place over generations, and will involve home and family life.

Hofstede's dimensions

Geert Hofstede's model of the dimensions of national culture was based initially on the results of an extensive research project that surveyed the employees of IBM in 50 countries (Hofstede, 2001). Analysis of the results initially identified four cultural dimensions: power distance, uncertainty avoidance, collectivism/individualism, masculinity/femininity, then at a later stage long-term/short-term perspective was added. Criticisms of Hofstede's model are identified and discussed in Chapter 1; in this chapter I will focus on explaining the dimensions themselves and their implications for information management.

It must be noted that Hofstede does not directly relate the management of information to the cultural dimensions. Of interest, though, are his comments relating to accounting in organisations. In general, he believes that the less an activity is governed by technical necessity, the more likely it is that it will be subject to cultural influences (Hofstede, 2001: 383). So, when considering accounting systems and acknowledging the fact that these systems are shaped largely by historical conventions, Hofstede concludes that it is logical for the rules of accounting and their use to vary along national cultural lines (p. 67).

A similar situation would seem to apply to information management, particularly to records and archives, but also to special library services. The next sections of this chapter consider each of Hofstede's dimensions in turn. In Hofstede's analysis, he developed tables for dimension showing the key differences for the extremes of each dimension in the workplace. I have used this data to compile characteristics relating to each dimension that are likely to impact on information management, i.e., anything that may affect the creation, control, flow, access, retrieval or storage of information.

Power distance

The issue underlying the power distance dimension is that of inequality. Within the organisational context, unless you are working in a very, very unusual setting, this is inevitable given employer/employee, manager/staff reporting lines. Positioning on this dimension indicates how this inequality is perceived by participants. Scores assigned by Hofstede to countries on the power distance index (PDI) were calculated on the basis of responses to three questions. These questions aimed to elicit attitudes of staff towards disagreeing with management (that is, whether or not employees are afraid to disagree with their manager), and actual and preferred decision-making styles of management (autocratic, persuasive/paternalistic or democratic) (Hofstede, 2001: 79).

Countries at the extreme ends of the power distance dimension are referred to as either high PDI or low PDI. Those at the highest end include Malaysia, Latin American countries, Arab countries, India, France and Hong Kong. Those at the lowest end include Britain, Australia, New Zealand, Scandinavian countries and Austria (Hofstede, 2001: 87).[1]

Hofstede summarised the key differences in work organisations between low and high power distance societies. In Table 2.2, I have selected only those that may impact on the management of information.

Organisational structure and management style differences

Most of these characteristics are to do with organisational structure and management style. These will undoubtedly impact on the ease with which information will flow within an organisation, and its accessibility to staff. For example, organisations situated in a high PDI society may have a predominately downwards one way flow of information from management to employees, where decisions are made at a high level and transmitted down to subordinate staff. There may be little sideways flow of information between organisational units, or upwards flow from employees to management.

In contrast, organisations situated in a low power distance society with the flat structure and consultative management style predicted by Hofstede (see Table 2.2) may have

Table 2.2	Work organisation differences in low and high PDI societies

Work organisations in low PDI countries are more likely to have:	Work organisations in high PDI countries are more likely to have:
Decentralised decision structures	Centralised decision structures
Flat organisation structure	Hierarchical organisation structure
Small proportion of supervisory personnel	Large proportion of supervisory personnel
Ideal boss who is resourceful democrat, sees self as practical, orderly, relying on support	Ideal boss who is well-meaning autocrat, regards self as benevolent decision maker
Managers relying on personal experience and on subordinates	Managers relying on formal rules
Subordinates who expect to be consulted	Subordinates who expect to be told
A view of consultative leadership as leading to satisfaction, performance and productivity	A view of authoritative leadership and close supervision as leading to satisfaction, performance and productivity
Innovations that need good champions	Innovations that need good support from hierarchy
Openness with information, also to nonsuperiors	Information constrained by hierarchy

Source: From Hofstede, 2001: 107–108.

information flowing upwards, downwards and sideways between management, staff and colleagues, but this may be in uncontrolled and erratic ways. The characteristic of openness with information may mean that the principle of freedom of access may be significant. It would be interesting to explore whether there is an association of freedom of information legislation with countries having a low ranking in terms of power distance. However, whether that translates to recognition of the need for appropriate infrastructure within organisations to manage information so that it is available is another matter entirely, as the case of New Zealand shows.

New Zealand has a very low ranking on the power distance index, and was one of the first countries to implement freedom of information legislation in 1982. However, this coincided with the drastic restructuring of the public sector and one of the casualties was records management. At this time many government agencies registry services were decentralised and records staff positions were cut. So there is a clear precedent for a cultural predisposition for openness with information not to be necessarily a good thing in terms of recognition of the need for information management in organisations.

According to Hofstede's study, high power distance is a characteristic feature of Chinese cultures and indicates that status is accorded very high importance. There is a significant body of literature by expatriate academics at Hong Kong universities which attempts to explain the Chinese culture to Westerners and the implications for business. For example, the psychologist Michael Bond's *Beyond the Chinese Face* describes how relationships within organisations will be governed by a strict hierarchy, based on Confucian tradition (Bond, 1991). He suggests that leadership roles in Chinese organisations will have wide-ranging authority which is not necessarily associated with accountability, and concludes that more decisions are made in private by fewer people in Chinese culture. High value will be accorded to power, wealth and expertise.

From my own experience conducting research in Hong Kong, interviews with staff in a university became very easy to organise when I was able to mention the name of a senior university executive. In one notable instance someone I needed to interview was fully occupied all week in training, but when I mentioned the name of the executive my interviewee immediately offered to be available after work hours. Another example of the importance of hierarchy was provided by features of the workplace. In the offices of the university it was evident that a lot of emphasis was given to defining and also making explicit the relationships between staff, and that the staff themselves were very conscious of those relationships. Outward signs of those relationships were displayed in the office accommodation and proximity of individuals to each other. At first sight the division appeared to be between managers located in offices, and the staff reporting to the manager in open-plan areas. However, the open-plan work areas were also divided, and workspaces ranged through a number of subtle configurations, from cubicle to shared desk. Also a person's status within the organisation was immediately obvious from the ranking assigned to their position title (clerical officer I, clerical officer II, and so on) and this was indicated in the internal telephone directory.

Similarly, at this university it was noteworthy that the webmaster reported directly to the President's Office. This reporting line was felt to be necessary because the web represented an enterprise-wide project. Therefore it had to be clearly demonstrated that the webmaster was relatively independent and would not have loyalty or give precedence to a particular work unit.

Reliance on experience and subordinates, versus rules

The characteristic in low PDI countries of reliance on personal experience and on subordinates suggests that decision making may be ad hoc, perhaps not documented, and furthermore that textual sources of information may not necessarily be preferred or regarded as authoritative.

When I visited the site of my Australian case study, the university was undertaking a large-scale project which aimed to rationalise and standardise all written policies and procedures. So work was underway to consolidate all policies into a single electronic resource, distinguishing between policies, procedures and guidelines, and determining a standardised format. This work was a topic raised by most interviewees, some viewed this as a positive development, and others were more doubtful. The consolidation process was described as being fraught with difficulty as it was found that many existing documents did not actually meet the criteria that had been established for policies. It is typical of a country where there is low ranking in terms of power distance that the development of written guidance was ad hoc in nature, and that it was necessary at a later stage to return and try to apply an overarching framework in order to organise this information.

Preferences for textual information are also further discussed below as a feature associated with 'Individualism/ Collectivism'.

Openness with information

Returning to the research undertaken by expatriate academics at Hong Kong universities, Ernest Jordan (1994) suggested that a characteristic of high power distance may be that 'management information may well be precisely that, information only available to management . . . Pressure may well be put on the information providers to generate only the information that is acceptable' (p. 13).

This emphasis on hierarchy and consequent importance of the manager or boss implies that relationships within a work unit will tend to be familial and supportive, with the downside being that there may well be inter-unit rivalry rather than collaboration:

Loyalties, being narrow, are rather more difficult to meld into an organization-wide affiliation. Usually their ambit is only as wide as the immediate boss's range of direct relationships. This consequence of paternalism often results in inter-departmental indifference, stone-walling and competitiveness in Chinese organizations. (Bond, 1991: 84)

The need to maintain the status quo is likely to have a negative impact on the keeping of information as evidence, for accountability purposes. The interests of managers are best served by 'maintaining prerogatives unfettered by systematic records or documented regulations' (Martinsons & Westwood, 1997: 223).

Attitudes to innovation

I have included Hofstede's characteristic of innovation in Table 2.2 as, given the ever-changing emerging trends in our digital environment, many information managers will be in the position of having to introduce innovations. In high power distance societies it will be necessary to have support for that innovation from the management structure; in low power distance societies a champion or crusader figure will be needed.

Uncertainty avoidance

The uncertainty avoidance dimension and associated scores on the uncertainty avoidance index (UAI) refer to uncertainty about the future and the extent to which a culture will attempt to minimise that uncertainty. Uncertainty avoidance was calculated using the answers to three questions – the questions addressed staff attitudes to company rules and regulations, employment stability and stress.

Countries which ranked highly in terms of uncertainty avoidance include Germany, Switzerland and Austria, those at the other end of the spectrum include the United Kingdom and China.

Hofstede has summarised the key differences in work organisations between low and high uncertainty avoidance societies. I have selected those that may impact on the management of information, and these are shown in Table 2.3.

Table 2.3   **Work organisation differences in low and high UAI societies**

Work organisations in low UAI countries are more likely to have:	Work organisations in high UAI countries are more likely to have:
Short average duration of employment	Long average duration of employment
Scepticism towards technological solutions	Bias towards technological solutions
Innovators who feel independent of rules	Innovators who feel constrained by rules
Renegade championing	Rational championing
Top managers involved in strategy	Top managers involved in operations
Power of superiors depending on position and relationships	Power of superiors depending on control of uncertainties
Tolerance for ambiguity in structures and procedures	Highly formalised management
Bias towards transformational leader role	Bias towards hierarchical control role
Innovations welcomed but not necessarily taken seriously	Innovations resisted but if accepted applied consistently
Employees who will have to learn and manage precision and punctuality	Employees to whom precision and punctuality come naturally
Relationship orientation	Task orientation
Belief in generalists and common sense	Belief in specialists and expertise

Source: From Hofstede, 2001: 169–170.

There is much in the profile of low uncertainty avoidance countries that presents significant challenges for information managers.

Short versus long-term employment

Leaving aside economic drivers to hang on to a particular job, cultural preferences are significant. A tendency towards preferring shorter duration of employment, together with ambiguity concerning procedures could mean that there is less chance of personnel being aware of information management policies and practice, or of following them. The archival scholar David Bearman has also speculated on the consequences of a low ranking in terms of this uncertainty avoidance dimension for information management. He describes methods of work in organisations where employment is likely to be of short duration as being strongly influenced by personal work styles, and where employees are judged by results rather than adherence to organisational practices (Bearman, 1992: 177). In today's digital workplace where most employees are likely to be creating and managing information at the desktop, tendencies to develop personal and unique working practices is a significant feature that needs to be recognised by information managers.

Attitudes to technology

Particularly interesting is the 'scepticism towards technology solutions' characteristic of countries with a low need to avoid uncertainty about the future that is identified in Table 2.3. It is certainly worth reflecting on given the user resistance to electronic documents and records management systems (EDRMS). Concerns about the effectiveness of these systems have been raised in Britain as a result of research undertaken by the National Archives (2009).

Specialists, expertise, rules and workflows

The existence of long-term employees, and a belief in specialists and expertise in organisations in countries that have a high ranking on the uncertainty avoidance index may signify respect for individuals as repositories of specialised and authoritative knowledge, but not necessarily negate a formal recordkeeping system. On the other hand, a low need to avoid uncertainty has been associated with a conclusion that rules and policy and procedural guidelines are less likely to be documented (Martinsons & Westwood, 1997). As explained in Chapter 1, documentation of policies and procedures is actively discouraged in the managerialist view of 'good' organisational cultures that has been very influential in western English-speaking democracies – precisely those countries which feature at the lower end of Hofstede's uncertainty avoidance dimension.

The accounting literature also presents some evidence of consideration of the influence of this cultural characteristic. Peter Smith (1992: 41) suggests that organisations in high uncertainty avoidance cultures are likely to have longer time perspectives and more structured decision-making procedures. Structured decision-making procedures imply very clear business processes and workflows, which are key prerequisites underpinning effective recordkeeping systems.

Jeffrey Cohen and colleagues (1993) discuss the relationship between the uncertainty avoidance ranking of a culture with ethical decision making on the part of auditors. They state:

> In general, auditors from strong UA cultures are more likely to equate 'legal' with 'ethical' responsibilities. In contrast, when specific legal sanctions are missing, those in low UA cultures might apply a broader ethical framework to decisions and refrain from questionable actions even if they were legal. (p. 5)

This implies that in countries with a high UAI ranking, accountability issues surrounding recordkeeping are less likely to be seriously taken into consideration if they are not also legal or regulatory requirements. Ethical considerations, if not based on legal requirements, might not even be considered as such. One confirmation of respect for regulation in high UAI societies comes from Frances Harvey (1997) who conducted an ethnographical study that compared the information systems design process in Germany and the United States. She describes how the German design process relied very heavily on standards, which is characteristic of countries with a high ranking on the UAI. That tendency has also been recognised in the archival literature: 'The Germans stick to the rules on *Aktenführung*. Like the Italians they use their ordinances and classification schemes as bureaucratic means to avoid uncertainty' (Ketelaar, 1997: 144).

Recognition of and respect for standards is of critical significance to information managers. The development of international standards is a strategy to provide a framework for information management in our complex digital environment; for example, ISO 15489 Records Management, ISO 23081 Records Management Processes – Metadata for Records and ISO 15389 Dublin Core Metadata Element Set. So an understanding of any inherent predisposition (or indeed resistance) to standards will help information managers in determining successful approaches to their implementation.

Organisational models – power distance and uncertainty avoidance relationships

Power distance and uncertainty avoidance characteristics are associated with distinct models or types of organisation. In countries where there is a combination of a high ranking on the power distance dimension with a high need to avoid uncertainty, the typical organisation type has been termed the 'full bureaucracy' or pyramid model (Hofstede, 2001: 377). As the name pyramid suggests, this organisation type is strongly hierarchical, and roles and functions will be clearly differentiated. It has been argued that technologies that promote and facilitate the dissemination of information in this organisation type would be implemented with considerable difficulty (Davison and Jordan, 1996). Full bureaucracies are most likely to be found in Latin, Mediterranean and Islamic countries, as well as Japan and some other Asian countries.

In contrast, in countries with a low ranking on the power distance dimension with a low need to avoid uncertainty about the future such as Britain, Australia and New Zealand, the typical organisation type will be implicitly structured, and is known as the market model (Hofstede 2001: 377). In this organisation type more importance is likely to be accorded to relationships between people than to rules and regulations (Mead, 1990: 26).

Although the cultural characteristics that define this organisation type may welcome technologies that enhance access to information, control aspects may not be so favourably received. As mentioned above, EDRMS may be particularly unsuited to this type of workplace. Not only do current manifestations of EDRMS necessitate work practices which may be perceived as additional burdens by the end user, but they also impose a formality which may appear at odds to informal, relationship-based working environment.

In my Australian case study, systems had been established for different functional areas, and sometimes for individual tasks within those functions, but little attention had been paid to the need for integration of those systems. Therefore there was no coherent way to manage information needed by different work units. There were, for example, no fewer than three quite separate information systems involved in the publication of course materials. All generated essential information, but all operated independently of each other.

The third type of organisation is the personnel bureaucracy, likely to be typical in countries characterised by a high ranking on the power distance dimension coupled with a low need to avoid uncertainty about the future. This has been termed the family model (Hofstede, 2001: 377). As this term suggests, this organisation type is centred on a strong leader whose authority is associated with the individual, rather than the rank or position which he or she holds. These organisations are likely to be found in China, India, Hong Kong and Singapore, for example. As with full bureaucracies, technologies that facilitate the dissemination of information may be regarded as a threat rather than a benefit in this organisation type.

The final organisation type is likely to be found in countries with a low ranking on the power distance dimension associated with a high need to avoid uncertainty about the future. This organisation type has been referred to as a workflow bureaucracy (Mead, 1990: 26) or more descriptively as a 'well-oiled machine' (Hofstede, 2001: 377). These organisations are most likely to be found in the German-speaking world of Germany, Switzerland and Austria. Here, in contrast to the market model, more emphasis is placed on regulating activities. This would seem to be the ideal organisation type in terms of accomplishing records management objectives. Theoretically there should be no major concerns about inhibiting or restricting access to information from a defending the hierarchy perspective. Furthermore, any well-oiled machine will have very clearly identified workflows which will facilitate the identification of activities that should result in the creation of records. The fluidity and lack of fixity associated with the market model is just not apparent here, a boon for records managers!

These four organisation types are applied to the scenarios described in the final chapter.

Individualism and collectivism

This dimension measures the degree to which a society views individualism as a positive or negative trait. Individualism index (IDV) scores were assigned after analysis of answers to 14 questions relating to work goals (Hofstede, 2001: 214).

Cultures are referred to as being individualist or collectivist, depending on their IDV ranking. The United States is the highest ranking individualist country, closely followed by Australia. Chinese and South East Asian countries are examples of collectivist cultures.

Key differences between individuals in low and high IDV societies have been summarised by Hofstede, and I have selected just a few of these as being the most relevant to information management. These are shown in Table 2.4.

However, these few characteristics are among the most interesting and could be crucial to successful information management in organisations.

Preferences for group versus individual work and views of information sharing

The first two characteristics reflect attitudes to sharing information which are fundamental to the ways in which people work in organisations positioned at the extreme ends of the individualist and collectivist dimension. The preference for working in small groups in collectivist cultures has a direct influence on the extent to which it is necessary and desirable to make information accessible.

The manifestation of these features in a collectivist culture was very apparent in the case study that I undertook of an

| Table 2.4 | Differences in low and high IDV societies likely to impact on information management |

Individuals/Work organisations in low IDV (collectivist) countries are more likely to have:	Individuals/Work organisations in high IDV (individualist) countries are more likely to have:
Employees that perform best in groups	Employees that perform best as individuals
A view of sharing information as an attribute of organisational success	A view of withholding information as an attribute of organisational success
Training at its most effective when focused at group level	Training at its most effective when focused at individual level
High context communication	Low context communication
Social network main source of information	Media main source of information
Lack of vertical integration in society	Vertical integration in society

Source: From Hofstede, 2001: 227, 228 and 244.

organisation in Hong Kong. Here, employees were very willing to share information with members of the same workgroup or team. When asked if they would willingly share work information with other teams, however, reactions were quite different. There was an expectation that if sharing information between workgroups was required this would have to be formally negotiated between the respective managers. Similarly, it was very noticeable that there was a lot of concern about allowing access to information. Information was to be protected, rather than made accessible. For example, when discussing archiving documents, the principal objection related to how to control access in the far distant future.

At this organisation there was no central server. The absence of this meant that not only was there no organisation-wide backup of data on personal computers, but also to collaborative work was not facilitated. The full functionality of groupware could not be used. For instance, staff could not organise meetings based on ascertaining individuals' availability as indicated in their electronic calendars.

Features that we may take for granted in one setting as being essential in order to work effectively may indeed be absent altogether in organisations in other cultural settings. The moral of the story being, of course, to find out why the situation exists in the first place rather than rushing in to implement information management features that may just not fit in with cultural attitudes.

Preferences for training delivery

This characteristic has been singled out because preferences as to how training should be delivered, on a group or individual basis, will have a direct impact on the effectiveness of that training. Information managers will inevitably have a responsibility to provide training, whether it is in the use of a new system or introducing new policy. Increasing the chances of successfully achieving changes in practice will be enhanced if cultural characteristics are taken into account.

High versus low context communication

Earlier in this chapter I introduced the Hall model of culture, based on a continuum of preferences to high versus low context. Hofstede has linked this theory with his individualist/ collectivist dimension, associating low context preferences with individualism, and high context with collectivism.

> High-context communication implies that little has to be said or written because most of the information is either in the physical environment or internalised in the person; only a small part is in the coded, explicit part of

the message. Low-context communication implies that the mass of information is made explicit. (Hofstede, 2001: 212)

Edward and Mildred Hall (1989) categorise Germans as low context – i.e., they need detailed background information when they interact with others, a historical perspective is useful and detailed background information is needed when making decisions. This implies that full and accurate recordkeeping is likely to be regarded as being of prime importance, and it is worth speculating on whether or not this characteristic will also impact on attitudes to metadata.

So, in low context cultures, information has to be made explicit and therefore there is likely to be a preference for textual information sources. In contrast, in collectivist cultures what is implicit in the context is equally, if not more important than, the explicit content. Therefore images are likely to be key tools used in communication. These preferences should be remembered in many areas of information management practice; for example, when determining what information should be prioritised for digitisation, or when designing training materials and instructional guides.

At my German case study organisation, each person I interviewed volunteered documentation (on paper and on CD-Rom) in order to supplement and support what he or she was saying. Documents included instructional guides for students, reports, public relations brochures, copies of curricula, copies of form letters and so on. All information sent out to students was also available from the university's website, but hardcopy would be handed over usually with the comment 'just in case you can't find it' or 'just in case you forget to look for this later'. Documents were detailed and factual, even when their purpose was promotional. The public relations-type brochure describing the university's virtual learning programme included comprehensive diagrams of the computer network, for instance.

Information gathering from social network versus media network

This characteristic is of great importance, particularly when designing library services. It indicates differences in the ways in which people in individualist and collectivist societies go about gathering information, at least initially. There has been very little academic research to explore this characteristic, but some speculation. For instance, preferences for information gathering from a media network have been described as people seeking business information from written resources: 'Whilst they will listen to the views of colleagues or relatives, they place much emphasis on the use of reading, reports, databases and information sources' (Morden, 1999: 21). Whereas people in collectivist cultures are more likely to trust social networks, whether in the family or at work, as sources of information.

Vertical integration

Another unexplored characteristic which is very significant for information management is what Hofstede (2001: 228) describes as the lack of vertical integration of members of individualist societies. This means that unlike collectivist cultures, people in individualist societies will not as a matter of course maintain links with their past. In Chinese societies, maintenance of those links with the past is reflected in the importance of genealogies. The tradition of compiling genealogies has existed for centuries, and this has not only been carried out by individual families but also by government bureaus (Zhao, 2001).

In individualist societies, however, names of ancestors will not necessarily be remembered through generations unless a hobby genealogist in the family makes a conscious effort to research their history. This need for research has led to what only can be termed the genealogical revolution in Western industrialised countries, which has had a profound effect on the nature and type of service provided by our memory institutions, particularly archives. This revolution has been brought about because of the sheer numbers of people researching their family history, their need to access records such as censuses, combined with the technological capabilities to digitise and make information globally available. It is easy for us in these Western countries, however, to assume that this is a universal phenomenon, but that is not likely to be the case. The impact of genealogy on memory institutions is not likely to be nearly so significant in collectivist cultures, where there are existing traditions of maintaining and preserving family histories.

Awareness and respect for the past is likely to have consequences for information management from a practical perspective. In Estonia (which has a medium ranking on the individualism scale) it was very noticeable that a high degree of importance was accorded to preservation issues, including the development of a national framework for action (Konsa & Reimo, 2009). I saw much more evidence of routine monitoring of environmental conditions (for example, recording of temperature and humidity) in libraries than I was used to seeing in New Zealand. Also there were signs that digital preservation challenges were being taken very seriously by archivists and records managers. Concern for preservation in itself seems to indicate looking both backwards and forwards in time. In other words, recognising the need to preserve information created in the past so that it can be accessed in the future.

Masculinity and femininity

This dimension measures the relative roles played by gender role values in a society. Hofstede explains as follows:

> I found both occupations and countries in the IBM data to differ along a social/ego dimension of work goals, opposing interpersonal relations goals (relationship with manager, cooperation, and friendly atmosphere) to ego-directed goals (earnings and advancement). This dimension is related to the percentage of women within the occupation or country sample, but is not accounted for by the varying shares of women only; we find it also in the responses by men in these occupations or countries. (Hofstede, 2001: 284)

Therefore masculinity and femininity *do not* refer to an individual's biological designation, but are used as relative terms to indicate cultural characteristics. Japan, most European countries and the United States are examples of 'masculine' countries. Scandinavian countries and the Netherlands are the most 'feminine'. Some of the differences in masculinity/femininity values (MAS) as summarised by Hofstede are shown in Table 2.5.

A direct relationship between this dimension and information management is not immediately obvious. The preference for problem solving by consensus in 'feminine' societies may, however, suggest that a very prescriptive approach to the management of information may not result in the desired outcomes. In other words, procedural changes should not be introduced to an organisation without appropriate consultation and debate. This dimension may therefore be significant when considering acceptance of, and compliance with, international standards of practice.

| Table 2.5 | Workplace differences in low and high MAS societies |

Employees in low MAS (feminine) societies are more likely to:	Employees in high MAS (masculine) societies are more likely to:
Work in order to live	Live in order to work
Value relations and working conditions as the key contributing factors to job satisfaction	Value security, pay and interesting work as key contributing factors to job satisfaction
Value equality, solidarity, and quality of work life	Value equity, mutual competition, and performance
Believe that managers are employees like others	Believe that managers are culture heroes
Believe that career ambitions are optional for both men and women	Believe that career ambitions are compulsory for men, optional for women
Undersell themselves when applying for jobs	Oversell themselves when applying for jobs
Resolve conflicts through problem solving, compromise, and negotiation	Resolve conflicts through denying them or fighting until the best 'man' wins

Source: From Hofstede, 2001: 318.

Long-term versus short-term

This final dimension was identified after the original IBM research project was completed. It emerged as a result of the Chinese Values Survey – a survey of students from 23 countries conducted about a decade after the initial study. The values addressed in the survey were suggested by Chinese scholars, in contrast to the IBM survey which was designed by Western researchers (Hofstede, 2001: 351).

Countries surveyed were ranked on a long-term orientation index (LTO) according to the relative degree of long-term/ short-term orientation in life. Out of 23 countries, China, Hong Kong and Taiwan demonstrated the highest long-term orientation, whereas Anglo-Irish heritage countries such as Australia, New Zealand, the United States and Great Britain showed a short-term orientation. As with the masculinity/femininity dimension, no features that appear significant for information management are obvious from a reading of Hofstede's discussion of this dimension. Which is not to say, of course, that it is not relevant to us, rather that it has not been investigated as yet.

Summary and conclusions

To conclude, negotiating access to the universities in Hong Kong, Australia and Germany to conduct research provides a very clear example of the ways in which national cultural characteristics can influence the flow of information within organisations:

The organisation type associated with Australian characteristics of low power distance and low need to avoid uncertainty is the market model, which is likely to place more reliance on personal relationships between employees than on rules and hierarchies (Mead, 1990: 28). The problems I experienced when attempting to negotiate access to the university in order to conduct the case study fitted with the characteristics of this model. The flow of information was erratic, subject, it seemed, more to the goodwill of individuals rather than systematic procedures. Communication was sporadic, and it was difficult to ascertain at times whether it was taking place at all. Decision-making bodies (such as the research committee) were in place and the rules associated with their functioning documented, but these rules were not necessarily known, or would not necessarily be sought out, by individual staff members.

In Hong Kong, finding out who to contact to request permission to carry out the case study was a straightforward two-stage process. The first person I contacted, an academic within the university, knew exactly who I should approach, and as soon as this person had given permission the project proceeded. There was no requirement to gain approval from any other body such as a human ethics committee.

In Hofstede's survey, Germany's ranking for power distance is relatively low, indicating that organisations are likely to have a flat structure and a consultative approach to management. The organisation type associated with German characteristics of low power distance and a high need to avoid uncertainty is the well-oiled machine model, the workflow bureaucracy. In this model, relationships between work processes are prescribed (Hofstede, 2001: 375), and therefore more emphasis is placed on regulating activities rather than relationships (Mead, 1990: 26). Communication is likely to flow up and down and outward from many points, but only according to well-defined procedures. The effectiveness of the information flow within the German university was confirmed by all interviewees, even though this organisation was distributed across a number of locations throughout the city. Negotiating access to the German university was the least problematic and the quickest to arrange. This was despite the fact that I had no knowledge at all of specific individuals who could point me in the right direction. My initial e-mail of enquiry was forwarded by university staff to the appropriate office, and actioned promptly. All interviews were scheduled for me, including the additional ones that I identified while onsite. Every assistance was provided to ensure that I would have minimal problems in keeping to the schedule, for example the information provided for me on arrival included relevant bus timetables.

Despite the dangers in relying on and applying national cultural models, there is much that will provide valuable insight to information managers in national cultural theory. The dangers lie in developing stereotypical ideas of behaviour and attitudes, and assuming that all individuals of a certain country will behave in the same way. The discussion of national cultural differences in this chapter must be interpreted in the context of likelihood, rather than certainty. Above all, exploration of these factors should encourage information managers to broaden their perceptions of a very wide range of preferences and attitudes to information, rather than narrow them.

Hofstede's cultural dimensions have been described in detail, and those features which seem relevant to information management explored. Differences in terms of power distance, uncertainty avoidance and individualism versus collectivism seem to be most significant to information managers. Regardless of whether you are working in a multi-national enterprise, on a collaborative project with team members spread across the globe or are serving a wide variety of users, there is much here that will be valuable to you. The English language professional literature is not surprisingly dominated by 'our' view of the world. This chapter has hopefully succeeded in pointing out that there is not just one such view that is applicable to all contexts. The following chapter considers other national features that may impact on information management, namely language, legislation and technological capabilities.

Note

1. Specific rankings for individual countries can be checked online at *http://www.geert-hofstede.com/hofstede_dimensions .php*.

References

Bearman, D. (1992) Diplomatics, Weberian bureaucracy, and the management of electronic records in Europe and America. *American Archivist*, 55(1), 168–81.

Bond, M. H. (1991) *Beyond the Chinese Face: Insights from psychology*. New York: Oxford University Press.

Cardon, P. W. (2008) A critique of Hall's contexting model – A meta-analysis of literature on intercultural business and technical communication. *Journal of Business and Technical Communication*, 22(4), 399–428.

Cohen, J. R., Pant, L. W., & Sharp, D. J. (1993) Culture-based ethical conflicts confronting multinational accounting firms. *Accounting Horizons*, 7(3), 1–13.

Davison, R., & Jordan, E. (1996) *Cultural factors in the adoption and use of GSS*. City University of Hong Kong Working Paper.

Fukuyama, F. (1995) *Trust: The social virtues and the creation of prosperity*. London: Hamish Hamilton.

Fukuyama, F. (2001) Differing disciplinary perspectives on the origins of trust. *Boston University Law Review*, 81(3), 479–94.

Hall, E. T. (1976) *Beyond Culture*. Garden City, New York: Anchor.

Hall, E. T., & Hall, M. R. (1989) *Understanding Cultural Differences*. Yarmouth, Maine: Intercultural Press.

Hampden-Turner, C. M., & Trompenaars, F. (1994) *The Seven Cultures of Capitalism*. London: Piatkus.

Harvey, F. (1997) National cultural differences in theory and practice. *Information Technology and People*, 10(2), 132–46.

Hofstede, G. (1997) *Cultures and Organizations: Software of the mind* (Rev. ed.). New York: McGraw Hill.

Hofstede, G. (2001) *Culture's Consequences: Comparing values, behaviors, institutions, and organizations across nations* (2nd ed.). Thousand Oaks, CA: Sage Publications.

Jordan, E. (1994) *National and organisational culture: Their use in information systems design.* City University of Hong Kong Working Paper.

Ketelaar, E. (1997) The difference best postponed? *Archivaria*, 44, 142–8.

Konsa, K., & Reimo, T. (2009) Preservation priorities: Red Book of Estonian publications, 1535–1850. *International Journal of the Book*, 6(1), 11–16.

Krumbholz, M., & Maiden, N. (2001) The implementation of enterprise resource planning packages in different organisational and national cultures. *Information Systems*, 26, 185–204.

Martinsons, M. G., & Westwood, R. I. (1997) Management information systems in the Chinese business culture: an explanatory theory. *Information and Management*, 32, 215–28.

Mead, R. (1990) *Cross-cultural Management Communication.* New York: Wiley.

Morden, T. (1999) Models of national culture – a management review. *Cross Cultural Management*, 6(1), 19–44.

National Archives (2009) Integrating information management into business processes: Project outcomes. *http://www. nationalarchives.gov.uk/documents/discussion.pdf.*

Smith, P. B. (1992) Organizational behaviour and national cultures. *British Journal of Management*, 3, 39–51.

van Oudenhoven, J. P. (2001) Do organizations reflect national cultures? A 10-nation study. *International Journal of Intercultural Relations*, 25, 89–107.

Zhao, Z. (2001) Chinese genealogies as a source for demographic research A further assessment of their reliability and biases. *Population Studies*, 55, 181–93.

3

The structural environment

Abstract: This chapter provides the context relating to the structural environment that impacts on information management in organisations. This includes language, technological infrastructure and the legislative environment. The main areas of legislation considered relate to privacy, the protection of personal information; copyright, the ownership of information; and freedom of information, the rights of citizens to access official information. This chapter does not attempt to provide definitive discussion of these topics, but merely sets out to establish the main features of each and to highlight those features which may influence the management of information in organisations.

Key words: legislation, privacy, copyright, freedom of information, legal deposit, archives legislation.

Introduction

The objective of this chapter is to specifically include national and regional factors that will be influential in shaping organisational cultures, but which may be missed if the focus is restricted to national cultural dimensions.

The need to take a holistic view of the political, legislative and social environment rather than restricting consideration to national cultural dimensions can be illustrated by looking at the example of Estonia, one of the Baltic states. Estonia has a long history of occupation by successive foreign powers (Denmark, Sweden, Germany and Russia), and for much of the twentieth century (1940–1990) was part of the Soviet Union (Raun, 2001). According to Hofstede's dimensions, Estonia's profile is very similar to that of Finland ('Geert Hofstede Cultural Dimensions'). A study of managerial values, however, found significant differences between these two countries (Alas et al., 2006).

In terms of industrial development, in relationship to other newly independent countries in Eastern and Central Europe, Estonia has been categorised as a high level medium adaptor (Hyder & Abraha, 2008: 293). These authors comment that Estonia is culturally closer to Sweden and Finland because of historical business and social links, and also that industry is doing well in terms of privatisation, adaptation and modernisation.

In 2004, Estonia became a member of the European Union. Regionally it is referred to as one of the Baltic states, thus is grouped with Latvia and Lithuania. Legislation relating to information management in Estonia appears to be accorded a high priority as archival and legal deposit legislation has been updated in recent years (Euronomos: European Archival Information Online, 2009; Suneksemplari Seadus, 2009). Given the amount of work required as a consequence of legislative changes following independence in 1991, the fact that these acts have received attention indicates a high importance accorded to these areas. Hong Kong was in a comparable situation in terms of the magnitude of change as the territory was handed back to China from Britain, but as will be seen later in this chapter the legislation enacted in the pre-handover period showed that information management concerns were not a priority.

Similarly, the existence and status of public policy relating to information management will vary according to country, reflecting different levels and areas of concern. Estonia provides an example of a state where explicit and well-documented policy has been developed relating to cultural heritage, both analogue and digital (Ministry of Culture, 2008). Preservation of that heritage is the focus of much attention and activity, as is evidenced by the 'Red Book' strategy (Konsa and Reimo, 2009). Public policy relating to the development of an information society post-independence is explored in depth by Runnel et al. (2009).

This brief snapshot of a country has used Estonia as an example to show the complex web resulting from, and continuing to be shaped by, historical and current relationships. All of these relationships will have some degree of influence over the way in which information is managed in organisations in specific countries.

Continuing our examination of the context that organisations are situated within, any consideration of their culture has to take into account the laws and regulations within which they operate. This chapter begins with consideration of the importance of language and technological infrastructure issues. It then provides an overview of the regulatory environment in general terms, and then considers three main areas in more detail: privacy, copyright and freedom of information legislation. These three are of critical importance to information management, and although the concepts are internationally applicable the manifestations of particular legislation varies greatly. Indeed, some researchers have suggested that national cultural characteristics are influential in shaping this environment. I will also consider the extent to which employees are aware of and accept the provisions of this legislation, as this is another important factor to take into account in assessing organisational culture.

Language

Language is a key factor that will need to be taken into account when considering organisational culture and the need to manage information. It is of course inextricably linked with culture, but it is worth singling out for separate discussion in order to emphasise information management consequences which may arise due to the use of different languages, and because of the implications of the use of different character sets for digital accessibility and sustainability issues.

Of particular interest are the differences between high and low context languages, which has been associated with variations in information-seeking behaviour (discussed earlier in Chapter 2). Research into high and low context differences appears to be largely limited to exploring Asian and Western comparisons (see for instance Li-Jun Ji et al., 2009) whereas there is considerable difference to be found even among European languages in the degree of context required. There is undoubtedly a need for much further investigation in this area, which has the potential to be very significant for information management.

Particular problems can be associated with languages based on non-Latin script. The international standard for character encoding (ISO 8859) for instance does not even include Chinese characters because of their complexity. Nevertheless, the use of standards for encoding to take into account diacritical elements in different languages is enormously important if there are aspirations to enable equal access to people speaking those languages. The Norwegian government has announced that the character sets used by public sector organisations have to conform to UTF8. This is to make sure that characters in Norway's minority language, Sami, and others can be displayed correctly.[1]

Requirements to use more than one language, and willingness to do so, will certainly influence information management concerns. Multilingual websites, for instance, dramatically increase possibilities to access information beyond national and linguistic boundaries. However, the complexity involved in ensuring that versions are up-to-date and translations are authoritative cannot be underestimated.

The small country of Estonia provides some insight into the defining nature of language, and the consequences of this for information management. Estonia's language policy is said to illustrate the importance of language in defining national identity (Rannut, 2004). The country's national awakening in the late nineteenth century was preceded by a steady increase in publications in Estonian and marked by the standardisation of a new writing system and acceptance of the Northern dialect as the national language (Raun, 2001). Towards the end of the Soviet occupation of Estonia in the 1980s, the status of the Estonian language was seen as a critical characteristic essential for the survival of the nation and its culture (Raun, 2001: 235). Changing relationships with other powers has influenced choices relating to other languages; most recently, English has become the preferred second language to be taught in schools. A consequence of this will be that direct access to primary information sources relating to the recent past will be more problematic if future Estonian citizens do not have the appropriate linguistic skills.

Regional technological infrastructure

The capability and capacity of the organisation's internal information technology systems will of course impact on the nature of information management services. But it is important to take a step back and consider the broader environmental context, because this dictates the opportunities and constraints that are the parameters for internal development. In addition, regional capabilities will influence the extent to which employees are restricted to working within organisational boundaries, their acceptance of organisational limitations and/or need to develop alternative solutions.

Today's social networking, or Web 2.0, environment offers a huge range of possibilities for alternative ways of working. When it is no longer necessary to be in a designated physical space in order to work, a whole range of issues that may make life much more complicated for information managers arise. People are able to log into their work systems such as e-mail and conduct business from remote locations. Voice-over-internet protocol software such as Skype enable real-time global communication. Computing in the Cloud, using cyberspace as a vast open-plan office and storage repository opens up possibilities for collaborative working alongside issues that are only now emerging, such as ownership and responsibility for data.

In addition, portable storage devices enable employees to carry vast amounts of data off work premises, and also of course raise huge risks in terms of loss and unauthorised access to information.

Underlying people's ability to take advantage of these features is the need for adequate equipment, power and access to information technology. There will of course be huge contrasts in the facilities available in western developed countries from those in third world and developing countries, on the other side of the digital divide. But some features of the Web 2.0 environment may enable digital working in ways not previously possible in countries without a robust technological infrastructure. Contrasts are also apparent among countries in the developed world, largely due to telecommunications policy and the associated infrastructure.

Free wireless internet makes a huge difference to the extent to which the flexibility of communication will be taken advantage of, and incorporated into working outside the bricks and mortar of traditional organisational boundaries.

Also, of course, it is important to bear in mind that if the regional technological infrastructure is one which facilitates the use of these new tools and features, organisational policy should reflect this reality. Otherwise the result may well be sabotage of internal information management systems. Whether this sabotage is intentional or accidental, the result will be the same as people develop their own workarounds.

I encountered an instance of the complexity of this new environment when consulting for a public sector organisation based on one of the island nations of the South Pacific. Internet bandwidth was limited, and an attempt to develop an online document repository that could be accessed remotely failed because download times were excessive. The organisation focused on developing approaches to restrict internet usage where possible, in order to make better use of the bandwidth that was available.

One of the results of this strategy was to ban the use of Skype, as this was viewed as software which presented an excessive drain on bandwidth. Furthermore, Skype was perceived as a tool that was used for social, rather than work purposes. However, employees had developed their own communication practices as an integral feature supporting and facilitating their work, and Skype played a central role.

The functions of this organisation meant that employees travelled a great deal, largely to Pacific island nations that were even more remote. One of the primary purposes of travel was to take part in meetings which involved high-level negotiation of policy spanning different jurisdictions. Skype was used wherever possible as a quick and easy way of checking back with colleagues and managers, especially to ensure that any decisions or positions taken out of the office were in keeping with home organisational policy. When Skype could no longer be used, employees developed their own workaround. This, in effect, consisted of making sure that the organisation's information could be accessed externally. Staff established their own personal e-mail accounts in the cloud, for instance setting up hotmail or gmail accounts. Then before travelling, they would e-mail themselves copious quantities of documents to make sure they could have them to hand if needed. This was in addition to using portable memory devices such as USB sticks, as people had found from experience that these small devices could easily be lost or left in someone else's computer. All in all, it was no understatement to say that the organisation's most important information resources were exposed to significant risks, largely due to insufficient attention being paid to understanding how information technology could be used to support work practices.

The regional technological infrastructure plays such a key role in shaping and influencing information management practices. It must be taken into account when developing policies, and that involves keeping up to date with the latest social networking tools and finding out how they are used within organisations. It is in many ways much easier to take a draconian approach to limiting the use of such tools, or banning the use of portable memory sticks, but the end result of such actions is highly unlikely to be beneficial to organisational information management.

Overview of the regulatory environment

As I have already noted, organisations do not exist in isolation. They are a microcosm of the environment in which they are situated, and will reflect the standards and norms of that environment, as embodied by the broader legislative framework. The functions of the organisation are a key factor in determining which legislation is applicable. For instance, information management in a hospital setting will be subject to rules and regulations regarding the prescription of drugs, the confidentiality of details relating to a patient's disease and its treatment, and the need for informed consent. Whether an organisation is in the private or public sector is also significant, as different legislation is likely to apply.

The type of legislation will vary according to the political structure of the country concerned, and any regional alliances. So, for countries such as Germany, Australia and the United States, which have a federal structure, there may be legislation at both state and national level. Membership of the country in international alliances such as the European Union will also have implications for legislation, introducing another layer of complexity.

It is also important to acknowledge the existence of standards which establish codes for best practice. Standards may be applicable internationally, nationally or be industry or sector specific. The best known standards are likely to be those that are international developed by the International Organisation for Standardisation (ISO). ISO is a non-governmental organisation made up of a network of 145 national standards bodies. It promotes the development of standards in order to facilitate the international exchange of goods and services, and develop international collaborative activity. Standards are used internationally in order to:

- make the development, manufacturing and supply of products and services *more efficient, safer and cleaner*;
- *facilitate trade* between countries and make it *fairer*;

- provide governments with a technical base for *health, safety and environmental legislation*, and conformity assessment;

- *share* technological advances and good management practice;

- disseminate *innovation*;

- *safeguard consumers*, and users in general, of products and services;

- make life simpler by providing *solutions* to common problems.

(International Organisation for Standardisation, 2010)

An ISO standard is the result of negotiation and agreement between national member bodies. The ISO website sets out the procedure for drafting and creating a standard. Development work is carried out by Technical Committees (TC) and their related Sub-Committees (SC), and is usually a six-stage process.

As I pointed out in Chapter 2, standards are increasingly becoming an important feature influencing information management, particularly in records management and electronic recordkeeping systems. Standards may also, of course, be applicable to the functions of the organisation, so it is essential that these are identified and any implications for information management taken into account when developing programmes and services.

The same comment also applies to legislation, of course. In this chapter I will focus on the features that are particularly important to information management across a wide range of sectors. Information managers will most definitely also need to ensure they are cognisant of the legislation that is applicable to the functions of their organisations, and be aware of any ramifications for their responsibilities. But that is beyond the scope of this book, so the remainder of this chapter will focus only on those areas which will have wide applicability for organisations in different sectors.

Privacy

Privacy requirements relate to the need to protect personal information about oneself or about other people. The extent to which privacy is protected by legislation varies from country to country. Similarly, the extent to which relevant laws or standards are recognised and adhered to by individuals will also vary greatly according to country.

When organisations operated on a very localised basis, simply becoming aware of the norms of that particular jurisdiction and then making sure that they were followed could be the primary concern for information managers. However, given the cross-border and global reach of today's information systems, the glorious complexity of the ranges of attitudes towards privacy, and corresponding variations in legislation, are very relevant to the work of information managers.

In fact, these variations in attitude are also apparent beyond formal organisational e-commerce systems, and are impacting on social networking spaces. The availability of personal information on Facebook and YouTube has prompted legal action from countries where there is a greater sensitivity to the need to protect personal information from exposure unauthorised by the person involved.[2]

The legislation

There are countries with no formal privacy legislation or rules for the protection of personal information at all, such as

Argentina, Thailand and Malaysia (Milberg et al., 2000). But even restricting our overview to those with privacy regulation, there is still a considerable diversity of models in place. The variation in legislation relating to the protection of personal information has been represented as a continuum of regulation. At one end of this continuum is the laissez faire of non-governmental intervention, at the other extreme is high governmental involvement and control (Milberg et al., 1995).

Sandra Milberg and colleagues identified five models of regulation along their continuum:

- *Self-help model.* As its name suggests, this model is the one with least involvement of government. Here, the onus is on the affected individual to protest any breach of rights, for example unauthorised use of personal details about them. Furthermore, the individual will have to bear any legal costs associated with upholding their rights. This model is said to be associated with France.

- *Voluntary control model.* In this model, the emphasis is on self-regulation by organisation, in accordance with legislation. A person is designated as the responsible officer within the organisation, to ensure compliance. The voluntary control model is in place in the United States and in Japan.

- *Data Commissioner model.* This is the half-way point on the regulation continuum. In this model, the regulation of privacy concerns is the responsibility of a government appointee similar to an ombudsman. This is the system that is in place in New Zealand, as well as in Australia and Canada. The work of New Zealand's privacy commissioner includes education and training, investigating complaints as well as monitoring uses of technology and reviewing new legislation for implications for privacy (Privacy Commissioner, 2010).

- *Registration model.* This is similar in intent to the licensing model (see below) in that a government body is set up for regulatory purposes, but actions are remedial rather than preventative. This is the model that is in place in the United Kingdom and Denmark.

- *Licensing model.* This is the strictest model and allows for full government regulation and intervention in order to protect personal information. This is the model that is in place in Germany.

Germany has a long history in terms of privacy legislation. The very first legislation relating to data protection was introduced in 1970, in the then West German state of Hesse. Some commentators have speculated as to whether attitudes to privacy can be associated with national cultural characteristics, in particular correlations between the power distance and individualist/collectivist dimensions (Walczuch et al., 1995). However, this high regard for the need to protect and guard access to personal information has also been associated with Germany's totalitarian past. In other words, memories of how personal information was used by the National Socialist regime for power and control made people in the former West Germany very cautious of, and aware of the possibilities for, misuse (Walczuch et al., 1995).

These attitudes can only have been reinforced subsequently by disclosures of the extent to which the State Security Service of the former East Germany (Staatssicherheitsdienst or Stasi) gathered information about citizens for the purpose of control. Targets for information gathering ranged from high-profile public figures in both the former East and West Germany to ordinary citizens. The scale of operations was such that, for the population of about 16.4 million individuals, there was one official employee per 180 citizens, plus over half a million 'unofficial employees' registered between 1949 and 1989 (BSTU, 2010). The dimensions of the type of information gathered went far beyond the sorts of data we may normally think about in terms of privacy and personal information, including attempts to capture people's individual scents:

> Mostly, smell samples were collected surreptitiously. The Stasi might break into someone's apartment and take a piece of clothing worn close to the skin, often underwear. Alternatively, a 'suspect' would be brought in under some pretext for questioning, and the vinyl seat he or she had sat on would be wiped afterward with a cloth. The pieces of stolen clothing, or the cloth, would then be placed in a sealed jar. (Funder, 2002: 8)

The German situation may be common to other totalitarian regimes, but it is particularly interesting because of developments after the breakup of the Soviet Union and the fall of the Berlin Wall. When it became clear that change to the ruling structure was imminent, the East German authorities attempted to dispose of the records relating to their surveillance operations. Masses of files survived intact, and after the reunification of Germany legislation was passed to enable access to these records, primarily for the purposes of Aufklaerung, personal clarification of the secret power that had controlled peoples' lives. Even those files that were destroyed by shredding are being re-assembled. Initially that was being done manually by a team of people – painstaking and laborious work indeed. Subsequently, however, technology has come to the aid and software has been developed to automate this process. In all, the resources directed to this activity are huge, and reflect the importance of this discovery process accorded by the German government.

However, this operation has prompted intense debate in Germany. The need to vindicate the personal rights of those people who were targeted for investigation cannot be done without disclosing the names of Stasi agents and informers and therefore infringing their rights to privacy. The scale of the surveillance activity undertaken by the Stasi was immense, with files accumulated on over six million people. That, of course, entailed a correspondingly large number of people tasked with gathering information. The procedures now for providing access to these files appear to have been developed in order to try to protect the identity of those informers, as the names of any other individuals mentioned are obliterated.[3]

Also keeping this debate alive in Germany is the reluctance by some high-profile members of the population to authorise disclosure to 'their' files. These include former ruling politicians such as the West German Chancellor Helmut Kohl. The controversy will undoubtedly continue, and similar situations are being enacted elsewhere in Eastern Europe where personal information was collected by the state for the purposes of power and control over citizens.[4]

People's attitudes to privacy

So history, politics and culture are all likely to be significant factors which influence people's attitudes to the importance of protecting information about themselves. In countries where there is less awareness of the potential for the use of personal information for power and control, even if relevant legislation exists, it may not be regarded as particularly important. In Hong Kong, for instance, before the return of this former British colony to China, a number of changes to legislation were introduced. (Negotiations preceding handover resulted in the agreement that the laws already in force in Hong Kong would be maintained so long as they did not contravene China's Basic Law (Conner, 1997: 94).) Among these new laws was one relating to privacy, the Personal Data (Privacy) Ordinance, which was based on British legislation. A brief overview of the objectives of this personal data ordinance at the time of its enactment (Lau, 2000), is noteworthy as it emphasises the contribution of the ordinance to Hong Kong's economic well being. It stresses that the introduction of this legislation will ensure that trade restrictions will not be imposed on Hong Kong by countries that do have data protection laws. In other words, the motivator for the legislation appears to be economic rather than the recognition of the need to protect the rights of individuals to restrict access to information about themselves.

A lack of recognition of the consequences for misuse of personal information can certainly be observed in the workplace, as I found in my study of information management in a Hong Kong university. Here, a data protection officer had been appointed in accordance with the recently enacted ordinance. The functions of this officer appeared to have been viewed by staff as rather tedious, but there was no suggestion that compliance would not be forthcoming. In this instance, then, very clear and explicit guidance and procedures would have to be provided as to what the requirements to protect personal information were, and there should not be any expectation that employees would necessarily understand why those requirements were being implemented.

By way of contrast, in the Australian university I studied there was certainly general awareness amongst staff of the need to protect and maintain confidentiality of the records relating to students. However, at the time of my visit the staff I interviewed could not actually find the university's policy and guidelines relating to privacy, but were confident that one did exist as privacy was such an important concern. So their default position, in the absence of specific guidelines, was to make sure that these records were kept securely and protected from unauthorised access.

Freedom of information

Freedom of information refers to the rules that guarantee access by citizens to the information held by governments. Once again, there are a wide range of different attitudes towards freedom of information, which can have the end effect of not actually realising the intent of legislation. This is a very important feature to be aware of for information managers working in organisations such as government departments and local authorities that are subject to freedom of information laws.

A characteristic I noted in the previous chapter in connection with low power distance was 'openness with information'. The implication of this is that in countries where Hofstede found a low ranking on the power distance dimension, there is a likelihood that people will be more predisposed to sharing information rather than keeping it secret. However, this does not seem to fit with the picture of attitudes to freedom of information legislation in Britain.

Britain is one of the last Western democracies to implement freedom of information legislation. This reluctance to legislate in favour of open government has also been noted in countries that were former British colonies. Hong Kong, for instance, still does not have any freedom of information legislation.

As noted above, a number of laws relating to information management were introduced in Hong Kong just prior to handover of the territory to the People's Republic of China. Freedom of information, however, was not addressed. In fact, Britain played a key role in preventing its introduction.

In Jonathan Dimbleby's account of the handover period in Hong Kong, specific mention is made of the Governor (Chris Patten) blocking attempts to introduce freedom of information legislation in Hong Kong, although reasons for this are not specified (Dimbleby, 1998: 251).

British archival academics Andrew Flinn and Harriet Jones have compiled a provocative collection of papers which explores whether a legislative mandate to access information has a negative impact on those creating records (Flinn & Jones, 2009). In other words, does the knowledge that their actions will be subject to public scrutiny inhibit public servants from formally recording discussion, debate and decisions. Sadly, there appears to be some evidence for this view from commentators around the world (Hannant, 2009; Schewe, 2009) notably including Sweden, which has a long and distinguished tradition of allowing public access to official information dating back to the eighteenth century (Östber & Eriksson, 2009). The Dutch contributor to this volume rejects this pessimistic view, however, and points to the introduction of desktop computing as the more significant factor causing 'empty archives' (De Graaff, 2009).

The situation in Britain now, as regards freedom of information from an information management perspective, is very intriguing. When the legislation was finally enacted, it was accompanied by a code of practice relating to records management. The code has the very best of intentions and certainly emphasises the need for effective records management if the aims of freedom of information legislation are to be realised:

> Any freedom of information legislation is only as good as the quality of the records to which it provides access. Such rights are of little use if reliable records are not

created in the first place, if they cannot be found when
needed or if the arrangements for their eventual
archiving or destruction are inadequate. Consequently,
all public authorities are strongly encouraged to pay
heed to the guidance in the Code. (*Lord Chancellor's
Code of Practice on the Management of Records,*
2002)

By accompanying the legislation with clear guidance as
to the essential information management infrastructure
required, it could be assumed that Britain would avoid the
situation in New Zealand mentioned in the previous chapter.
New Zealand can be regarded as an early adopter of freedom
of information among Anglophone countries as this
legislation was introduced in 1982, replacing the existing
Official Secrets Act. However, there was minimal recognition
of the need for records management services in order to
effectively respond to requests for official information. On
the contrary, this period of time can be characterised as a
time of crisis for records management, as registries were
dispersed and records management positions lost in so many
government departments (Oliver & Kurmo, 2010).

However, the situation in Britain today indicates that even
if there had been high-level recognition of the need for
records management to support freedom of information
requirements, it still might not have had the desired result.
Elizabeth Shepherd and colleagues have conducted research
exploring the impact of freedom of information legislation in
local authorities in Britain. They conclude that, despite the
rhetoric, records management still may not be regarded as
particularly important in these organisations:

. . . whilst superficially FOI seems to have facilitated a
change in the perception of records management, how

deep the culture change has actually been and how far it has penetrated organisations beyond the front-end customer interface can be questioned. (Shepherd et al., 2009: 238–239)

I cannot escape from the view that even though legislation might be in place, even though explicit codes of practice might be issued, people's attitudes and values to information will still be instrumental in influencing successful information management. It is of enormous importance for records managers in particular to recognise this, and not to assume that the intent and purpose of freedom of information legislation will be upheld if appropriate policy is developed. On the contrary, if there is a fundamental resistance to freedom of information ideals and aspirations, there may well be disastrous consequences for organisational and even national memories. Much more research is needed to answer the 'empty archives' question posed by Flinn and Jones. In the meantime, however, awareness of this potential problem area will assist information managers to be particularly vigilant and emphasise the importance of creating and maintaining full and accurate records.

Another feature worthy of consideration is maintaining an openness as regards the format and media of those records. If, as Bob De Graaff suggests, technology is a prime influencing factor, perhaps records managers should be considering alternative ways in which records should be created, such as audio and video recordings. This of course would in turn present many challenges in terms of managing this information so that it was retrievable and could be stored for long periods of time. The consequences of continuing with current practice, regardless of whether or not desired outcomes are achieved, does not seem to be an acceptable option.

Copyright

Copyright legislation can be defined as the rights of ownership accorded to authors and creators of information. These rights govern the extent to which copying and distribution of information can take place. The protection of copyright lasts for a certain period of time, after which the information object passes into the public domain. The period of time varies from country to country, as does the starting point for the applicability of relevant legislation, and the range of formats that it is applied to.

The digital environment has vastly complicated requirements relating to copyright as reproduction, copying, extracting portions of a work to incorporate into new work become easier and easier. Mash-ups, the compilation of bits and pieces of different information types (such as sound, image, graphics as well as text) to make a new digital information resource does not require expensive equipment or even necessarily specialist expertise. The potential therefore for copying and profiting from someone else's original work without acknowledgement is indeed great.

This situation creates obligations for information managers to ensure that organisational resources are used appropriately. The first step of course is to make sure that you are familiar with requirements in order to provide appropriate guidance. This is no small task, as copyright more than any other area of legislation impacting on information management seems to be beset by myths and legends rather than a clear grasp of facts. This reflects the complexity of the environment and the high profile accorded to breaches of copyright in some countries.

Once again, cultural considerations are likely to result in different attitudes towards the ownership of information. Tim Padfield, a British copyright expert specialising in matters relating to unpublished materials, identifies two distinct approaches to copyright legislation. On the one hand is the British approach, also exported to the USA and commonwealth countries, which regards copyright as an economic property right. On the other hand, most other European countries take an approach which emphasises the protection of the author's personality, as expressed in the work (Padfield, 2010). Harmonisation of British copyright law with European Union legislation has taken place to ensure consistency of approach. However, given the quite different philosophical perspectives as regards the motivation for protection, it seems that people's instinctual knowledge as to what copying behaviours are permitted is likely to vary considerably according to country.

Furthermore, Padfield notes that despite the existence of international conventions (such as that administered by the United Nations World Intellectual Property Organisation) and the European directives, there are not only still considerable variations in legislative requirements within Europe, but also far more variations in countries outside Europe. He points in particular to variations in the definition of the copyright owner, which means that 'quite different people qualify as owners of copyright in the same work in different countries' (Padfield, 2010: 12).

All this adds up to the need to be aware that common understanding of copyright regulations, the motivation for copyright protection and the extent to which restrictions apply will vary widely among staff in organisations. Copyright infringements in the workplace therefore cannot be assumed to be of malicious intent, especially if there is not a high degree of public awareness of the need to protect the rights of information owners and when adequate guidance has not been provided by information managers.

Further complicating factors are the steps taken by copyright owners to protect their property, in the form of digital rights management. Digital rights management is the implementation of controls to guard against unauthorised use or copying. This technology may hamper preservation efforts if it is attempted, for instance, to migrate content to a more stable or long-lasting format. For instance, a library cannot assume ownership of the content of digital media as it may not be accessible in the future because of technological obsolescence.

It is not only essential, therefore, to become familiar with copyright regulations which exist in your jurisdiction, but also to maintain awareness of international developments. These may well influence the long-term availability of digital information resources that you may regard as being owned by your organisation, but which in fact may only be temporarily accessible. The debate surrounding the ownership of information will be ongoing, and solutions that emerge are unlikely to be universally applicable.

Conclusion

This chapter has been very wide ranging, covering what I have termed the structural environment in which organisations operate. The characteristics of the languages that are used, whether information needs to be made available in more than one language, and preferences for low or high context communication will all impact on information management. The technological capabilities and capacity of the region in which the organisation is situated and does business with have to be taken into account when developing information management policies and procedures within the organisation. Finally, the features of the regulatory environment, and whether staff are aware of their obligations let alone willing to follow them are essential characteristics which frame and shape organisational cultures. The following chapter moves on to consider the next layer of the organisational culture onion: occupational culture.

Notes

1. Ministry of Government Administration, Reform and Church Affairs: *http://www.regjeringen.no/eny/dep/fad/press-centre/press-releases/2009/new-obligatory-it-standards-for-the-stat.html?id=570650.*
2. See, for example, discussion following the announcement of an European Union investigation of the impact of tagging on privacy: *http://www.law.georgetown.edu/cleblog/post.cfm/european-privacy-regulators-investigate-tagging-features-of-facebook-and-google.*
3. Procedures are set out on the website of the government agency established to provide access to the files of the state security service of the former German Democratic Republic: *http://www.bstu.bund.de/cln_012/nn_1138150/EN/Inspection__of__files__and__examinations/Private__individuals/private__individuals__node.html__nnn=trueLdoc1138148bodyText6.*
4. See, for example, the website of the Rumanian National Council for the Study of Securitate Archives: *http://www.cnsas.ro/engleza/mission.html.*

References

Alas, R., Ennulo, J., & Tuernpuu, L. (2006) Managerial values in the institutional context. *Journal of Business Ethics*, 65, 269–78.

BSTU (2010) The Ministry for State Security (MfS) – Summary. *http://www.bstu.bund.de/cln_012/nn_710358/EN/Ministry__for__State__Security/ministry__for__state__security__node.html__nnn=true* (accessed 1 Sept 2010).

Conner, A. W. (1997) Legal institutions in transitional Hong Kong. In M. K. Chan (ed.), *The Challenges of Hong Kong's Reintegration with China* (pp. 85–111). Hong Kong: Hong Kong University Press.

De Graaff, B. (2009) 'The Access to Information Shuffle: Historical Researchers Versus the Government in the Netherlands'. In Flinn, A., & Jones, H. (eds.), *Freedom of Information. Open Access, Empty Archives?* London: Routledge, pp. 77–89.

Dimbleby, J. (1998) *The Last Governor: Chris Patten and the handover of Hong Kong* (2nd ed). London: Little, Brown.

Euronomos: European Archival Information Online (2009) Legal framework for the administration and management of records and archives, from *http://euronomos.euronomos.org/nuxeo/nxdoc/default/5ab772fe-6be4-4fc2-b730.-b877cfe51bdc/view_documents?tabId=&conversationId=0NXMAIN2&conversationIsLongRunning=true.*

Flinn, A., & Jones, H. (eds.) (2009), *Freedom of Information. Open Access, Empty Archives?* London: Routledge.

Funder, A. (2002) *Stasiland*. Melbourne: Text Publishing.

Geert Hofstede Cultural Dimensions. From *http://www.geert-hofstede.com/hofstede_dimensions.php.*

Hannant, L. (2009) 'Access to information and historical research: The Canadian experience. In Flinn, A., & Jones, H. (eds.), *Freedom of Information. Open Access, Empty Archives?* London: Routledge, pp 125–39.

Hyder, A., & Abraha, D. (2008) Institutional factors and strategic alliances in Eastern and Central Europe. *Baltic Journal of Management*, 3(3), 289–308.

International Organisation for Standardization (2010) *What Standards Do. http://www.iso.org/iso/about/discover-iso_what-standards-do.htm.*

Ji, L.-J., Tuo, T., Zhang, Z. & Messervey, D. (2009) Looking into the past: Cultural differences in perception and representation of past information. *Journal of Personality & Social Psychology*, 96, 761–69.

Konsa, K. and Reimo, T. (2009) Preservation priorities: Red Book of Estonian Publications, 1535–1850. *International Journal of the Book*, 6(1), 11–16.

Lau, S. (2000) *The Hong Kong personal data (privacy) ordinance*. Paper presented at the Proceedings of the tenth conference on computers, freedom and privacy: challenging the assumptions, Toronto, Ontario.

Lord Chancellor's Code of Practice on the Management of Records (2002) *http://www.foi.gov.uk/reference/imprep/codemanrec.htm*.

Milberg, S. J., Burke, S. J., Smith, J., & Kallman, E. A. (1995) Values, personal information privacy, and regulatory approaches. *Communications of the ACM*, 38(12), 65–74.

Milberg, Sandra J., H. Jeff Smith and Sandra J. Burke. (2000) Information privacy: Corporate management and National regulation *Organization Science*, Vol. 11, No. 1, pp. 35–57.

Ministry of Culture (2008) *Estonian Cultural Strategy 2008– 2011. www.kul.ee/webeditor/files/strategy_2008-2011.pdf*

Oliver, G., & Kurmo, K. (2010) *Dismantling bureaucracies and technological change: impacts on recordkeeping and the influence of organizational culture*. Paper presented at I-CHORA 5, London, 1–3 July.

Östber, K., and Eriksson, F. (2009) The problematic freedom of information principle: The swedish experience. In Flinn, A., & Jones, H. (eds.), *Freedom of Information. Open Access, Empty Archives?* London: Routledge, pp. 113–24.

Padfield, Tim (2010) *Copyright for Archivists and Records Managers*, 4th edn. London: Facet.

Privacy Commissioner (2010) *What we do* from *http:// www.privacy.org.nz/what-we-do/.*

Rannut, M. (2004) Language policy in Estonia. *Noves SL: Journal on Sociolinguistics. http://www6.gencat.net/ llengcat/noves/hm04primavera-estiu/docs/rannut.pdf.*

Raun, T. U. (2001) *Estonia and the Estonians* (2nd updated edn.). Stanford, CA: Hoover Institution Press.

Runnel, P., Pruulmann-Vengerfeldt, P., & Reinsalu, K. (2009) The Estonian tiger leap from post-communism to the information society: from policy to practice. *Journal of Baltic Studies*, 40(1), 29–51.

Schewe, D.B. (2009) Access to information: Promise versus practice in the USA. In Flinn, A., & Jones, H. (eds.), *Freedom of Information. Open Access, Empty Archives?* London: Routledge, pp. 90–101.

Shepherd, E. et al. (2009) The impact of freedom of information on records management & record use in local government: A literature review. *Journal of the Society of Archivists*, 30(2), 227–48.

Suneksemplari Seadus (2009) Electrooniline Riigi Teataja from *http://www.riigiteataja.ee/ert/act.jsp?id=968385.*

Walczuch, R. M., Singh, S. K., & Palmer, T. S. (1995) An analysis of the cultural motivations for transborder data flow legislation. *Information Technology and People*, 8(2), 37–57.

4

Occupational culture

Abstract: This chapter considers the second layer of the organisational cultural model, occupational culture. The characteristics of the occupations or professions that people belong to will influence the way that they work with information, so it is important for information managers to be aware of the potential for very different values, attitudes and approaches. The occupational culture of librarians and recordkeepers is also discussed, and the consequences of these sometimes competing cultures on our overall objectives of managing information.

Key words: occupations, professions, warrant.

Introduction

The objective of this chapter is to explore the middle layer of our organisational culture model, i.e. occupational culture. Occupational culture refers to those values and practices which have been learned in the course of vocational education and training. The chapter therefore begins by defining the main features relating to occupational culture and uses the example of a university setting to illustrate how the different attitudes to information on the part of two broad groupings of employees will impact on information managers. The final part of this chapter considers occupational culture from the inside, with a view to determining what influence our occupational cultures as librarians, archivists and records managers have on information management.

Occupational culture

To define occupational culture we can return to the Dutch anthropologist Geert Hofstede (whose definition of the characteristics of national culture has been used in Chapter 2). His theory includes consideration of those distinct cultural characteristics which reflect the values and identity associated with a specific occupational group, rather than country. He suggests that

> ... entering an occupational field means the acquisition of both values and practices; the place of socialization is the school or university, and the time is between childhood and entering work. (Hofstede, 2001: 414)

In other words, the values acquired in the process of education and training for a particular occupation will overlay those cultural characteristics acquired from home and family. The timing indicated by Hofstede in the above quote of course assumes a very traditional career pathway where one selects an appropriate occupation after completing formal education early in adulthood. However, I do not think that non-traditional approaches to careers, i.e. commencing study for a particular job later in life, invalidates the concept of distinguishing occupational cultural characteristics. Despite the fact that working life is increasingly characterised by changing direction, and second-chance learning enables professional qualifications to be gained at a much later stage than immediately post-schooling, cultural characteristics associated with occupations will still be influential.

Consideration of subcultures within organisations such as those associated with particular occupational groups shows that these can be widely divergent – simply working for the same organisation does not imply that the same values and practices will be shared (Hofstede, 1998). Based on Raelin (1986), Hofstede proposed six dimensions of occupational culture:

1. Handling people versus handling things

2. Specialist versus generalist

3. Disciplined versus independent

4. Structured versus unstructured

5. Theoretical versus practical

6. Normative versus pragmatic. (Hofstede, 2001: 415)

Occupational culture has received far less attention in the literature than either national or corporate culture (Hofstede et al., 1990). Edgar Schein (1996) suggests that occupational communities generate cultures that not only cut across organisations, but also nations – i.e., an occupational community will develop similar worldviews. He goes on to explain that:

> The shared assumptions derive from a common educational background, the requirements of a given occupation such as the licenses that have to be obtained to practice, and the shared contact with others in the occupation. (p. 12)

One of the main articles cited which explores the impact of occupational cultures in organisations is by Australian academics Geoffrey Bloor and Patrick Dawson. They describe how new employees will learn appropriate behaviours from various sources, including official documentation and managers, but also from external reference groups such as professional colleagues working elsewhere and trade unions (Bloor and Dawson, 1994: 278). The focus of Bloor and Dawson is on professionals, and the impact that professional subgroups have on the organisational culture. They describe the effect of these interactions as complementing, conflicting and counterbalancing the primary culture. Bloor and Dawson emphasise that professionals are more likely to regard other members of their profession as their primary reference group, rather than colleagues who are not members of that same professional group. This is because members of the same profession share a distinct pattern of values, beliefs and behavioural norms, as well as similar understandings or interpretation of each other's actions (Bloor and Dawson, 1994: 283). Professional associations, of course, play a key role in ensuring that values, beliefs and norms are maintained and upheld, often by formulating a code of ethics.

More recently, British researchers Adrienne Curry and Caroline Moore (2003) state that harmonious co-existence between professional groups can be threatened when faced with change:

> If change is such that the organization itself is perceived to be under threat, sub-cultures will tend to be ignored in favour of the need for organizational cohesion. If, however, there is no perceived threat to organizational survival, sub-cultures are more likely to close ranks and revert to a strong identification with their profession. (p. 97)

This is a crucial point which needs to be taken on board by information managers working in organisations that include occupations that are clearly defined, and represented by a professional or industry association. Given the rapidly developing digital environment, information management strategies are likely to include the implementation of systems and processes that may fundamentally affect the way in which people work. In other words, be disruptive and represent profound change. So the introduction of, for instance, an electronic document and records management system may signify change of significant magnitude that members of professional groups within the organisation close ranks and resist implementation.

Occupational culture and information behaviours

Although there has been far less research into occupational culture than national culture, its relationship with information and knowledge sharing has been investigated. A study of occupational cultures (in government agencies that is scientist, politician and bureaucrat roles) concluded that these subcultures are very influential in driving information sharing needs and behaviours (Drake et al., 2004). Another very relevant study found variations in awareness of national information and communication technology policies among different professional and sectoral groups in Egypt (Meso et al., 2006).

Research into information-seeking behaviour has explored variations according to occupation. The legal profession in particular has been the subject of much interest with respect to information seeking and use of electronic resources (see Richards, 2009 for a bibliography of empirical research studies).

The impact of occupational culture on information management in a university

Universities provide vivid examples of complex environments where there are a number of distinct occupational cultures all contributing to shaping the overall organisational culture, and often in competition with each other. First there are two broad groupings, which, despite attempts to present a unified face to the outside world, can represent a deep division within the organisation. These two groups are the academics on one hand and administrative staff on the other. Although both groups are essential in order for the university to carry out its functions and activities of teaching, learning and research, interactions are often adversarial rather than complementary.

Secondly, within each group there are many further divisions. Academics are divided on the basis of discipline, which can result in vastly different approaches to carrying out fundamental activities. Research by a humanities scholar will use completely different methodologies and tools to those used by a biochemist for instance. Differences between disciplinary perspectives are so profound that these academic subcultures have been referred to as tribes, jealously claiming ownership of their own territories (Bacher, 1989).

The scale and scope of universities are such that the broad grouping of administrative staff will be similarly complex, even if relationships between occupations are hopefully not as visceral as the inter-disciplinary rivalries that characterise the academics. Which camp a particular occupation or profession falls into may vary according to university policy – librarians, for instance, in some countries may have academic status, and in others be part of the administrative group. In summary, occupational cultures will play a very important role in shaping the overall organisational culture of a university.

The potential for occupational cultures to influence information management has recently been highlighted for me as I have attempted to set up a research project which involves analysis of university records to find out what literature was used in the reading lists for management education in New Zealand in the 1980s. The universities in this country do not have a good history of recognising the need for records management and archives. Priorities have changed drastically, though, as a result of new legislation (Public Records Act 2005) which, for the first time, established accountability on the part of universities and polytechnics to create and maintain public records.

However, specifically excluded from the scope of the legislation are some records relating to teaching and research, which results in guidance carefully specifying that the Act only applies to 'certain records' (Archives New Zealand, 2010). So when I set about trying to find out whether the records I needed to access for my research were available I met with brick walls at every turn. The response from each university was that it was not possible to say whether the information I needed was available, it would be a question of contacting the academic department concerned and trying to find out whether individuals had maintained their own records.

This situation not only suggests that future historians will have major problems attempting to find out the detail of what was taught in our universities, but also provides a glimpse into the challenges faced by those people attempting to manage records in this environment. The exclusion of teaching materials used by academics and research data from the scope of the Public Records Act would not have been a decision that was taken lightly. A possible explanation is that establishing requirements to create and maintain full and accurate records was viewed as a threat to academic freedom. In other words, a threat to one of the core values and principles of the academic profession. The end result, of course, is that the core activities undertaken by this group of employees remain firmly outside the sphere of influence of information managers.

Our occupational cultures

Whether information managers can identify a distinct occupational culture is debatable. Consideration of this demonstrates just how poorly defined and fuzzy the concept is. One characteristic of occupational culture is a shared educational background. However, the extent to which that premise can be applied to information managers varies internationally. Kajberg (2002) has noted that in education for library and information studies within Europe there is little commonality.

> In spite of increased communication and networking efforts, pooled expertise and joint experience, spectacular results in terms of demonstrable synergy effects, action plans, development projects, co-ordinated curricular structures, joint ventures, joint degrees, established equivalence of qualifications, etc., are few. (p. 166)

Maceviciute (2002) analysed information management programmes of study in institutions in three specific regions: the Baltic countries, Nordic countries and the United Kingdom. She documents a bewildering array of offerings, at both postgraduate and undergraduate level, with curricula covering at least one of these disciplines: library studies, records management, archival studies, possibly in conjunction with each other and possibly in conjunction with other disciplines. Also interesting is the range of affiliation of programmes in the United Kingdom, ranging from faculties of arts to engineering (p. 196). Ellis and Greening (2002) review the provision of educational programmes for archivists in Europe, Canada, United States and Australia, and note the active involvement of professional bodies in this regard in Canada and North America, in contrast to the United Kingdom. The UK is also out of step with other countries in attempting to provide entry-level training in just one year at postgraduate level. Other countries offer a variety of entry points, including undergraduate, and the programmes are longer in duration.

Literature exploring professional identity issues of information management professionals also sheds some light on occupational culture. This is an area where there is a lot of anecdotal evidence and discussion, but little research. Librarians in particular show concern about their image and there are numerous articles and websites that attempt to repudiate a perceived image of conservatism (see, for instance, *http://www.librarian-image.net*). The introduction to a special issue of the North American journal *The Reference Librarian* devoted to the topic remarks:

> It seems that every profession has a natural interest in its universal image and a tendency toward self-examination. For example, the engineering profession is particularly concerned with licensing and qualifications, the medical profession pays special attention to credentials and training . . . For all of this professional navel-gazing, there seems to be no profession as preoccupied with self-examination as that of librarianship. While some of

it may stem from an identity crisis, the refrain heard over and over is startlingly similar to Dangerfield's 'I don't get no respect'. (Arant & Benefiel, 2002: 1)

A review of images of librarians from the eighteenth century to today shows that the librarian's image has generally been shaped by subjective opinion or description of general personality trait, for example 'accessible, friendly, skilled, altruistic' (p. 21), and stereotypes of 'the scholarly, resourceful professional; the timid, plain-looking, middle-aged female; the passive gatekeeper' (p. 21).

The article concludes that today the image of a librarian is as unclear to librarians themselves as it is to others, due to the environment of transition and uncertainty in the virtual information age, and consequent uncertainty relating to the role of a librarian (Church, 2002).

Rothstein cites 'numerous' studies of the librarian personality type and states that there has been general agreement on personality traits: 'Extreme deference, submissiveness, respect for authority, conscientiousness, orderliness, conservatism, lack of self-confidence' (Rothstein, 1985: 46).

He further characterises librarians as tending to be anxious and self-critical. A survey of users of two special libraries in the United Kingdom found that the perception of librarians was of people who are

efficient, intelligent and helpful, possessing specialised knowledge, and undertaking a range of tasks beyond the routine and traditional. They are seen as unambitious people, whose satisfaction is in helping others to achieve their ends. (Fleck & Bawden, 1995: 222)

The staff of the libraries surveyed generally seemed to concur with this user perception, which leads Fleck and

Bawden to warn against low self-image. This has been noted as a problem for librarians by other authors (Atkinson, 1994; Cram, 1991; Fourie, 2004; Rothstein, 1985; Schuman, 1990).

Librarians protest their image, but they are at least a familiar occupation to the public. Archivists and records managers are not so well known. Richard Cox and David Wallace have suggested that archivists and records managers need to strive towards achieving an 'archive literacy' for both the public and policy makers so that people understand what it is recordkeepers do, and why it matters (Cox & Wallace, 2002: 8). Ann Pederson points out that, in the new world of Australia and North America, most people have minimal knowledge of records work. She attributes this to the fact that recordkeeping is largely subsumed by the work it supports, and furthermore that there is no comparative formative educational experience involving recordkeeping agencies in the same way as libraries or museums (Pederson, 2003). Pederson surveyed Australian archivists to determine temperament type, using a Myers-Briggs Type Indicator survey instrument. She found that the majority of Australian archivists belonged to the Guardian temperament group, the strengths of which are

- logistics-procurement, distribution, service and replacement of *materiel*, i.e. stuff, but not of people or systems;
- hard-working, respectful, dutiful, modest, tenacious;
- maintain stability, continuity, traditions;
- accurate, reliable, trustworthy;
- procedures, rules, detail;
- integrity and concern to 'do right' in the real world.

She concluded that

archivists possess in abundance the personal attributes essential for workplace effectiveness. However, while some of these qualities are acknowledged, most are either unrecognised or improperly deployed because our own modesty and dedication to the job keep ourselves, as well as others, from exploiting our strengths. Because we are poorly understood, we are, like our records, 'organisationally invisible' and therefore at the mercy of the vicious old stereotypes of archivists as caretakers in the boneyard of information and recordkeeping as mere 'filing'. (Pederson, 2003: 260)

A distinct occupational culture for the three professional groups involved in information management does not appear from the literature, although each of the three serves the needs of their host institution. A concern for public awareness of the scope, nature and complexity of each occupation is apparent. What does start to become clear from each sector's published literature is at least an element of uncertainty as to the future for the three occupational groups, some confusion as to identity, and a need perhaps for more self-awareness of roles within information management, and of responsibilities to organisations and society.

Why this matters is because perceived occupational differences may hamper or impede our work as information managers. Where there is competition for jurisdiction between existing occupational groups, such as is currently evident within information management, cultural interactions will add to the complexity and challenge of the issues that are faced.

An example of the consequences of the influences of occupational culture in our domain is provided by a case study of the work of the committee responsible for drafting the international standard on records management,

ISO15489. I undertook this case study because reports documenting the development process suggested that the inordinate length of time required to draft the document was a result of national cultural differences (for instance, Steemson, 2001a,b, 2002).

I spent three days observing the work of the committee, and interviewing members. One of my main goals was to find out why everything had taken so long. The committee functioned as a community of practice, the lengthy and often difficult processes of negotiation leading to an understanding of points of difference, if not acceptance. The length of time taken to draft the international standard, given that it was based on an existing document, is indicative of the lack of a pre-existing shared understanding and language in this particular domain.

It appeared that national cultural differences in isolation were not the major source of problems, rather that the differing occupational cultures of records managers and archivists were the principal barrier to achieving consensus. However, those occupational cultures were inextricably linked to national cultures, as there was a clear divide on national grounds between countries where records management has been accepted as a separate system, from those where 'archives' represented both the management of current and archival records. The complexity, though, of cultural influences was emphasised by the fact that within 'mixed' national delegations composed of the two occupational groups, there were tensions between the representatives.

National differences were also evident, particularly in legislative requirements, conflicting views as to whether the standard should be mandatory or not, in the attitude of countries towards participation in standard-setting, and in preferences relating to the language, format and style of the published document. Differences were manifest in problems experienced in communication and in approach to organisational rules and norms. Conversely, similarity of values as regards the masculinity dimension may have contributed towards the length of time necessary to achieve consensus. In need of investigation is analysis of non-participating countries and whether the reasons for non-participation may have been occupationally or nationally based.

Conclusion

Organisational culture theorists agree that occupational cultures are significant and can be extremely influential. Very little, however, is known about them, particularly in the context of information management. Determining which occupational groupings are present within an organisation, and being prepared for significant behavioural differences, is important for information managers. Consideration of the occupational cultures of information managers themselves adds further complexity, but awareness of differing and possibly conflicting professional goals may be enlightening.

References

Arant, W., & Benefiel, C. R. (2002) *The Image and Role of the Librarian.* New York: Haworth.

Archives New Zealand (2010) *Universities: Information for New Zealand universities* from *http://www.archives.govt .nz/advice/public-offices/universities.*

Atkinson, J. (1994) The image of the academic librarian: an analysis of the implications for the future through a study of the literature. In C. Harris (ed.), *The New University Library* (pp. 89–100). London: Taylor Graham.

Bacher, R. (1989) *Academic Tribes and Territories: Intellectual enquiry and the cultures of disciplines*. Milton Keynes, SRHE and Open University Press.

Bloor, G., & Dawson, P. (1994) Understanding professional culture in organizational context. *Organization Studies*, 15(2), 275–95.

Church, G. M. (2002) In the eye of the beholder: how librarians have been viewed over time. In W. Arant & C. R. Benefiel (eds), *The Image and Role of the Librarian* (pp. 5–24). New York: Haworth.

Cox, R. J., & Wallace, D. (2002) Introduction. In R. J. Cox & D. Wallace (eds), *Archives and the Public Good: Accountability and records in mordern society* (pp. 1–18). Westport, CT: Quorum.

Cram, J. (1991) Self love and joy and satisfaction in librarianship. *Australasian Public Libraries and Reference Service*, 42(2), 75–81.

Curry, A., & Moore, C. (2003) Assessing information culture – an exploratory model. *International Journal of Information Management*, 23, 91–110.

Drake, D. B., Steckler, N. A., & Koch, M. J. (2004) Information sharing in and across government agencies: The role and influence of scientist, politician and bureaucrat subcultures. *Social Science Computer Review*, 22, 67–84.

Ellis, M., & Greening, A. (2002) Archival training in 2002: between a rock and a hard place? *Journal of the Society of Archivists*, 23(2), 197–207.

Fleck, I., & Bawden, D. (1995) The information professional: attitudes and images. Examples from information services in law and medicine. *Journal of Librarianship and Information Science*, 27(4), 215–26.

Fourie, I. (2004) Librarians and the claiming of new roles: How can we try to make a difference? *ASLIB Proceedings*, 56(1), 62–74.

Hofstede, G., Neuijen, B., Ohayv, D. D., & Sanders, G. (1990) Measuring organizational cultures: a qualitative and quantitative study across twenty cases. *Administrative Science Quarterly*, 35(2), 286–316.

Hofstede, G. (1998) Identifying organizational subcultures: an empirical approach. *Journal of Management Studies*, 35, 1–12.

Hofstede, G. (2001) *Culture's Consequences: Comparing values, behaviors, institutions, and organizations across nations* (2nd edn). Thousand Oaks, CA: Sage Publications.

Kajberg, L. (2002) Cross-country partnerships in European library and information science. *Library Review*, 51(3/4), 164–70.

Maceviciute, E. (2002) Information management in the Baltic, Nordic and UK LIS schools. *Library Review*, 51(3/4), 190–9.

Meso, P., Checchi, R. M., Sevcik, G. R., Loch, K. D., & Straub, D. (2006) Knowledge spheres and the diffusion of national IT policies. *Electronic Journal on Information Systems in Developing Countries*, 23(3), 1–16.

Pederson, A. (2003) *Understanding Ourselves & Others: Australian archivists & temperament. Archival Science* 3(3), 223–74.

Raelin, J. A. (1986) *The Clash of Cultures: Managers and professionals.* Boston, MA: Harvard Business School Press.

Richards, R. (2009) Legal information systems and legal informatics resources: Information behavior (selected), from *http://home.comcast.net/~richards1000/LegalInformationSystemsBibliography.htm.*

Rothstein, S. (1985)Why people really hate library schools. *Library Journal*, 110(6), 41–8.

Schein, E. H. (1996) Three cultures of management: the key to organizational learning. *Sloan Management Review*, 9–20.

Schuman, P. G. (1990) The image of librarians: substance or shadow. *Journal of Academic Librarianship*, 16(2).

Steemson, M. (2001a) *ISO15489: Set it to music. You're gonna need it!* Retrieved 7 Jan 2003 from *http://www. caldeson.com/hobart01.htm.*

Steemson, M. (2001b) *World taken by surprise: Nations agree the best "how to's".* Retrieved 7 Jan, 2003, from *http://www.caldeson.com/techr011.html.*

Steemson, M. (2002) *RM standard ISO15489 takes the world by storm.* Retrieved 7 Jan 2003 from *http://www. caldeson.com/1548902.html.*

5

Corporate culture

Abstract: This chapter considers the most superficial layer of organisational culture: corporate culture. This cultural layer is the one that is the most susceptible to change, and it reflects those characteristics or artefacts which are unique to that particular organisation. These include management style, in-house language and stories, dress code, interior design and external branding.

Key words: corporate culture, management, interior design, narratives, branding.

Introduction

The purpose of this chapter is to explore the final and most superficial layer of the organisational culture 'onion': corporate culture. Corporate culture is the concept that is most commonly misrepresented as constituting the entirety of organisational culture, as discussed in the first chapter. In general, the characteristics that are unique to specific organisations reflect corporate culture, and this layer is the one that is most susceptible to change. That susceptibility to change is a very misleading factor. It leads people to assume that change to corporate culture will be instrumental in shifting and modifying the much more deeply rooted values and beliefs that constitute organisational culture. The chapter begins with a short recap of corporate culture from the perspective of management theory, and then discusses the artefacts that may reflect corporate culture, such as management style, in-house language, employee dress code, interior design, and external representation (name, logos, website design, publications).

Corporate culture – the tip of the iceberg

As discussed in the first chapter, the view of organisational culture taken by some management theorists focuses solely on the superficial characteristics that are unique to individual organisations. This is the domain that is identified in this book as corporate culture. Because the characteristics of corporate culture are so unique, there are inherent difficulties in trying to describe a universal model, let alone attempt to implement change in order to impose an idealistic and probably unrealistic organisational culture. However, what can be done is identify which characteristics or artefacts are likely to reflect corporate culture.

The notion of a 'good' or 'strong' organisational culture as proposed by Peters and Waterman (1982) is a fallacy. The problem is, though, that the very simplicity of this notion makes it very appealing. As we have established in the preceding chapters, organisational culture is strongly influenced by much more deeply rooted factors than the easily modifiable features such as developing new external imagery to represent the organisation. The consequences of attempting to implement change based on the faulty notion of just being able to construct and implement a brand new organisational culture is shown in the following example.

In New Zealand in 2001 an attempt was made to transform the culture of a public sector organisation. The setting was a very large, newly established department of central government, which was formed as a result of a merger between two existing entities: the Income Support Service and the New Zealand Employment Service. University of Otago academic Joe Wallis describes the situation which eventually led to an employment court case brought by the former chief executive of this government department, Christine Rankin. Wallis claims that Ms Rankin was appointed initially because she was expected to provide the transformational leadership necessary to reshape the organisation's culture (Wallis, 2002: 61). Attempts to achieve that cultural change included a series of roadshows (the department was highly dispersed throughout New Zealand):

> The 'roadshows' were essentially training events in which Rankin played a starring role as she focused attention of staff on an organizational vision and challenged them to commit themselves to strive toward its realization. At one of these events, Rankin herself was lowered onto the conference floor where she performed a 'Power in the Profession' dance while a background screen showed pictures of Gandhi, Martin Luther King and Christine Rankin. (Wallis, 2002: 64)

Excesses such as this, of course, drew the attention of the media and were not well received by the public, particularly given that these displays seemed to be fundamentally at odds with the mission of the organisation, namely administering the social welfare infrastructure for New Zealanders. Eventually Ms Rankin's contract as Chief Executive was not renewed, hence the employment court case. This case study is quoted here for two reasons. First, in order to emphasise just how crucial organisational culture is perceived as being in terms of acting as a barrier to change. Secondly, this case provides a striking example of a feature that reflects corporate culture: management style.

Management style

The extravagant and flamboyant management style of Christine Rankin reflects the values and attitudes of the leadership of that organisation, and can be viewed as a key characteristic of the corporate culture. Although this is an extreme example, it is generally not that difficult to determine the distinguishing features of management style. It may be reflected in the personality type of managers throughout the organisation: those promoted or appointed are likely to reflect desirable characteristics as perceived by executive leadership. It is a key feature that is extremely susceptible to change, as it is closely linked to individual preferences and behaviours.

For information managers it is important to be able to respond appropriately to whichever management style currently predominates. Attempting to represent information management concerns in ways which do not resonate with senior management can be extremely detrimental, especially in cultures that do not have a clear perception of the inherent value of the need to manage information. Where there is a flamboyant management or leadership ethos there may not be an appreciation of the need for a comprehensive and robust information management infrastructure. After all, our ideal systems are ones which function effectively and efficiently to seamlessly support and promote the work of the organisation, so by their very nature are likely to be low profile. In this case it would be advantageous to collect vivid narratives or anecdotes that demonstrate service effectiveness. For example, horror stories of the consequences for management of not being able to access information required to respond to media queries. Every organisation has these horror stories; the alert information manager should be documenting these and using them when appropriate.

The next suggestion discusses these narratives, as they are in themselves artefacts of the corporate culture.

In-house language and narratives

In contrast to management style, the development of an organisation's own language and the use of stories or anecdotes to communicate defining moments of an organisation's history are artefacts of corporate culture that are generally formed from the bottom up. In other words, they are not imposed or dictated from above, but occur naturally and organically.

The 'language' that develops within an organisation consists of the unique, in-house jargon that is used to refer to concepts and tools that are core to organisational functions. The uniqueness of the terms used may mean that they are not easily understood by outsiders. Own languages may be reflected in many different ways, for example the use of spoken acronyms or initialisms to refer to functions, activities or organisations. Sometimes the reason for the terminology used is no longer apparent, as it is linked to the historical development of the concept or tool. For instance, San Jose State University School of Library and Information Science refers to its course syllabi as 'greensheets'. These greensheets are web resources, created by faculty staff inputting the required details into online templates. They are called 'greensheets' because they were once distributed on green paper, now an antique artefact. (San Jose State University School of Library and Information Science, 2010.) The fact that this terminology has survived a complete change of format and medium is perhaps evidence of the significance of the task of developing a greensheet, and certainly demonstrates a shared understanding amongst employees of what is signified by this word.

The stories that circulate within an organisation can provide insight into values, attitudes and beliefs. They will often feature individual employees or managers playing key roles. Any factual basis for them may be tenuous to say the least, but the fact that particular events are significant enough to be repeated over time can provide insight into corporate culture characteristics.

These tales, myths and legends that circulate within an organisation have been referred to as 'corporate folklore' (Gabriel, 1991). Indeed, research into this rich mine of information has also included consideration of organisational humour and jokes as well as insults. Joanne Martin (2001) reviews the literature relating to organisational humour and warns that a distinguishing characteristic is that the humour is usually distinctly unfunny to outsiders! As for the insults, this fascinating area of study has been invoked in research into workplace bullying (Salin, 2003) and employee harassment (Guerrier and Adib, 2000).

Where these topics are particularly of interest to information managers is their ability to provide insight into how their service is perceived within the organisation. For instance, is the in-house filing system regarded as a joke? Does being assigned to help out in the school library signify reward or punishment? Being aware of where and how information management services figure within the corporate folklore can greatly assist in determining appropriate courses of action. If, on the other hand, services do not feature at all within the corporate folklore, that should probably be taken as a cause for concern, and consideration be given as to how to raise the profile of information management. As established in the previous section, stories or narratives should be used wherever possible to effectively demonstrate the consequences of poor information management.

A recent example that I encountered on a consultancy assignment was the loss of a founding document, one with great symbolic significance. This document was signed by government leaders from many countries, and was the formal record of the multinational agreement necessary to support the activities of the organisation. Copies of the document were certainly in existence, and probably could easily be obtained from the countries involved. However, the embarrassment and loss of face involved in doing that would have tarnished the image of the organisation. This anecdote provided the information manager with a valuable and useful tool to support the establishment of a business case for the development of managed storage for inactive records. However, this type of story should only be leveraged for internal purposes as there is there is great potential for damage to the organisation's reputation if leaked externally.

Visual cues inside the organisation

Simply by looking around inside the organisation it is possible to gather data regarding corporate culture. Observing the clothes that staff wear, the way that offices are designed and furnished as well as noting any naming patterns that are used may provide useful background information.

The way that employees dress will reflect the norms established by management as being acceptable for the conduct of the organisation's business. Dress codes, even if not explicitly stated, can range from the very formal to the very casual, laissez faire. Where dress codes are formalised by being documented in organisational policy they will often incorporate standardised uniform items which may be adopted in order to meet with health and safety requirements. Even in these cases, observation and analysis of the colours and styles of uniforms may be useful, as these are likely to reflect an image that is promoted or desired by management.

In the absence of any clear occupational health drivers, and/ or environmental concerns such as inadequate heating, the types of clothes worn by staff may be indicators of values and attitudes. Taking note of whether or not male employees, for instance, routinely wear a collar and tie or favour jeans and t-shirts may provide clues as to the likelihood of in-house regulations and procedures as regards information management being taken seriously. But the important caveat here is to stress that the interpretation should be in the broader context taking into account national and occupational cultural influences.

The interior design of an organisation may reflect the vision or aspiration of management as to their preferred corporate culture. Open-plan offices for instance have long been the subject for study, although Joanne Martin notes that organisational culture researchers have not often used this predominately psychological and sociological body of literature (Martin, 2001: 85). A recent study of a Dutch corporation provides an interesting analysis of the ways in which both interior and exterior building design reflect desires for corporate change (van Marrewijk, 2009).

Office design, particularly space utilisation and office furniture will often reflect attempts to address or change information-related behaviours. This is where a much more nuanced understanding of organisational culture is invaluable. As we established in Chapter 2, willingness to share information with colleagues (and whether those colleagues are solely those who are members of the same team or workgroup) is strongly influenced by national cultural characteristics, and so attempts to change attitudes and behaviours simply by implementing a certain physical working environment are not likely to meet with much success.

In a New Zealand organisation I worked in, an attempt was made to increase staff efficiency and promote organisational information management by prohibiting the purchase of certain office furniture. The items on the banned list were two- or three-drawer vertical filing cabinets for use by individual staff members. The only employees permitted to have filing cabinets were those in administrative support roles, and these were shared cabinets with lateral shelving. This led to much discontent amongst other employees, who certainly did not change their work routines as intended. Despite the ruling, people found alternative means of storing the paperwork they felt necessary to have at hand to do their work. Eventually, several years later, after a change in management, the original rationale for prohibiting the purchase of filing cabinets had been completely lost sight of and the policy was abandoned. The intended goal of sharing organisational resources, ensuring that only current information would be used for decision making was never achieved. In fact, the converse probably happened with staff feeling the need to hoard their own information, storing it in makeshift containers and 'secret' locations.

This type of situation can be seen as analogous to the types of inappropriate and draconian measures implemented in attempts to control digital information, as discussed in Chapter 3. Attempting to ban personal filing cabinets probably sounds absurd; this should be remembered when discussion turns to banning the use of memory sticks or access to cloud computing. These strategies to manage digital information have just as much likelihood of succeeding as the banning of filing cabinets did in the paper world.

Another manifestation of corporate culture may be detected in the names used for locations such as rooms or buildings within the organisation. These will range from being informative – e.g. a numbered code designed to reflect the relationship of buildings to one another to symbolic names. For example, a new European university recently renamed its constituent buildings. The original set of names reflected the subjects studied in those locations, for instance 'L Block' was the home of the language school. The new names were quite different, and did not appear to have much practical utility at all. The names selected were in Latin, with a tenuous connection to the geographical positioning of the buildings. Thus 'mare' was used for the building facing the sea, 'silva' for the building closest to woodland, and so on. These names were not likely to have been selected because of their utility in assisting students and staff find locations, but for their connotations. Latin was the traditional language for university education in this part of Europe, and by using Latin names a connection with illustrious traditions would have been established despite the fact that the university itself was founded comparatively recently.

Considering this in terms of corporate culture, the deliberate selection of this naming convention can be interpreted as a desire on the part of management to demonstrate high value accorded to the history and tradition of education, and a desire to convey a close relationship between this history and the current activities of the university. This certainly suggests a receptive environment for archival endeavours, and most definitely should be taken advantage of by an alert information manager.

External representation

How the organisation chooses to present itself to the external environment can reveal a lot in terms of corporate culture. Accordingly, analysis of relevant artefacts can be very illuminating. Relevant artefacts are likely to include those developed for corporate branding, such as logos, as well as other features associated with external dissemination of information such as websites and corporate hardcopy publications. The image that is portrayed may be deliberately constructed (i.e. if specialist expertise is utilised to design a brand) or may be more organic, if responsibilities are not specifically assigned. In both cases, decisions made as to how the organisation is represented will reflect priorities of management, and thus provide insight into corporate culture.

Conclusions

Much of what has been discussed in this chapter is often taken to represent the entirety of organisational culture, particularly management style and organisational image. Some authors refer to these superficial characteristics as 'organisational climate' (see for instance Allen, 2003) which conveys to those of us in temperate parts of the world just the right mixture of susceptibility to change and uncertain predictability.

Corporate culture can be analysed by observation of various characteristics and artefacts. These include the style of management and/or leadership, the stories and anecdotes that circulate, the use of in-house specialist language, and visual cues relating to interior design, dress and external representation. Careful reading of corporate culture will assist information managers by providing tools to use such as appropriate horror stories to support business cases.

The following chapter consolidates the layers (national, occupational and corporate) and structural influences (language, the regulatory environment and technological capabilities) on organisational culture identified thus far and presents an overall framework to assess an organisation's information culture.

References

Allen, D. K. (2003) Organisational climate and strategic change in higher education: organisational insecurity. *Higher Education*, 46(1), 61–92.

Gabriel, Y. (1991) On organisational stories and myths: Why it is easier to slay a dragon than kill a myth. *International Sociology*, 6(4), 427–42.

Guerrier, Y. and Adib, A. S. (2000) 'No, we don't provide that service': The harassment of hotel employees by customers. *Work, Employment and Society*, 14, 698–705.

Martin, J. (2001) *Organizational culture: Mapping the terrain*. Thousand Oaks: Sage Publications.

Peters, T. J., & Waterman, R. H. (1982) *In Search of Excellence: Lessons from America's best-run companies*. New York: Harper & Row.

San Jose State University School of Library and Information Science (2010) Greensheets. *http://slisweb.sjsu.edu/ facultyhandbook/progcourses/greensheets.php*.

Salin, D. (2003) Ways of explaining workplace bullying: A review of enabling, motivating and precipitating Structures and Processes in the work environment. *Human Relations*, 56(10), 1213–32.

van Marrewijk, A. H. (2009) Corporate headquarters as physical embodiments of organisational change. *Journal of Organisational Change Management*, 22(3), 290–306.

Wallis, J. (2002) Evaluating organizational leadership in the New Zealand public sector in the aftermath of the Rankin judgement. *International Review of Administrative Sciences*, 68, 61–72.

Further reading

Brophy, P. (2009) 'Narrative in organisations'. In *Narrative-based practice*. Farnham: Ashgate, pp. 103–30.

Gabriel, Y. (1998) An introduction to the social psychology of insults in organizations. *Human Relations*, *51*(11), 1329–54.

6

Assessing information culture

Abstract: This chapter focuses on the concept of information culture and how to apply this idea to your own organisation in order to identify particular problem areas and to work out appropriate solutions. A three-level framework for assessment is outlined, and the characteristics of each level are described. Suggestions are provided in order to use this tool in an organisation to diagnose its information culture.

Key words: information culture, trust, sharing information, information-related competencies, information literacy, information governance.

Introduction

Back at the start of this book I introduced the concept of information culture. Every organisation, no matter how large or small it is, regardless of its type and function, wherever in the world it is situated, has an information culture. Understanding the organisational culture is critical in working out which features characterise the organisation's information culture. This chapter considers how to tease out exactly those characteristics which will define the organisation's information culture. The chapter begins by outlining an overall framework to use for assessment, then describes each level of this framework, suggesting how to go about collecting the data necessary to compile a holistic picture of information culture. Armed with this information, you will then be able to identify and prioritise areas for action.

Framework for assessment

In the same way that we have established that organisational culture consists of multiple layers, information culture is shaped by influences occurring at different levels – some of which are more open to change than others! So I have developed a framework for assessment, which takes this into account. The framework is shown in the following table:

Level One	The base or fundamental layer can be assessed by consideration of:
	■ **Respect for information as evidence**. Recognition and awareness of the need to manage certain information for the purposes of accountability.
	■ **Respect for information as knowledge**. Recognition and awareness of the need to manage certain information for the purpose of increasing knowledge and awareness.
	■ **Willingness to share information**. The level of granularity to which information sharing is regarded as the norm within the organisation.
	■ **Trust in information**. This will focus on consideration of preferred primary sources for information, for example individuals or text resources.
	■ **Language requirements**. There may be constraints associated with particular character sets used and also the need for multilingual versions of information.
	■ **Regional technological infrastructure**. The technological infrastructure in place externally will be a profound influencing factor on the dimensions of the information culture within an organisation.

Level Two	*Skills, knowledge and experience related to information management, which can be acquired and/or extended in the workplace:* ■ Information-related competencies, including information and computer literacy. ■ Awareness of environmental (societal and organisational) requirements relating to information.
Level Three	*The third and uppermost layer is reflected in:* ■ The information governance model that is in place. ■ Trust in organisational systems.

Each of these levels is discussed in the following sections, together with suggestions as to how to gather data for assessment.

Level one

This level is the base or fundamental layer of an organisation's information culture. It would be very difficult, if not impossible, to effect any change at this level, but understanding of its dimensions is critical in order to make sure that the information strategies you do develop are appropriate for the organisation and will be adopted. This level has the largest number of features that need to be taken into consideration, beginning with respect for information managed for the two key purposes that will be the focus of records managers, archivists and librarians. The remaining characteristics at this level are all linked to the location of the organisation, whether they are associated with national culture (willingness to share information, trust in information) or structural features (language, technological capabilities).

Respect for information as evidence. The extent to which it is accepted within the organisation that certain information needs to be managed for the purposes of accountability provides the measure by which you can ascertain the degree of respect for information as evidence. This can be assessed by answering the following questions:

- Is there an organisation-wide filing system for current records?
- Are there professional staff employed to undertake records management?
- If an organisation-wide filing system exists, does it encompass all records, regardless of format and media?
- Does management consider that recordkeeping should be part of everyone's roles?
- Do employees throughout the organisation consider recordkeeping to be part of their responsibilities?
- Are systems and procedures in place to ensure that records are retained only as long as necessary?
- Is the organisation aware of requirements to identify, protect and preserve records of archival value?
- Are there policies and procedures in place to archive records, either in-house or by transferring to a designated archival repository?

Some of these questions can be answered simply by observation and identifying relevant policies. Others will need more work, in particular the question relating to employees' attitudes towards recordkeeping. In this case, it will be important to collect data from staff, either by interview, focus group or by constructing a questionnaire.

If all these questions can be answered with an emphatic and unambiguous 'yes', then the organisation shows a high respect for information as evidence. The more negative the responses, the lower the respect that is accorded to managing information for accountability purposes.

If there is very little existing activity relating to the management of current and archival records, then this does not mean of course that the relevant infrastructure cannot be introduced. But you will need to be aware that the need to promote and justify records management will be an ongoing concern; it should never be assumed that records management will be routinely recognised as being a good thing. This is particularly the case where employees in the organisation do not recognise the need to take responsibility for recordkeeping as part of their workflow.

Respect for information as knowledge. The extent to which it is accepted within the organisation that certain information needs to be managed for the purpose of increasing knowledge and awareness provides the measure by which you can ascertain the degree of respect for information as knowledge. This can be assessed by answering the following questions:

- Is there an in-house library?
- Are library services used by employees to inform their work?
- Are there professional staff employed to manage information for knowledge and awareness?
- If professional librarians are employed, does the scope of their responsibilities extend beyond a physical library?
- If a library exists, does it have sufficient funding to buy necessary information resources?
- If a library exists, does it have sufficient space to house resources?
- Are employees encouraged to ensure that their work is informed by consulting a variety of information resources?
- Do employees routinely go beyond Google when searching for information?

If all these questions can be answered 'yes', then the organisation shows a high respect for information as knowledge. The greater the number of negative responses, the lower the respect that is accorded to managing information for the purposes of increasing knowledge and awareness. In those cases it could be important for professional information managers to demonstrate expertise by getting involved in any other information projects within the organisation that are underway, such as intranet development. Here, professional skills can be applied to organising and structuring information, and linking to relevant external resources. It becomes important to show that information management is not something that is simply a feature of what may be thought of by staff as a very narrow and perhaps outmoded entity, a library, but is applicable in ways that can meaningfully support the organisation's activities.

Willingness to share information. The level of granularity to which information sharing is regarded as the norm within the organisation is the third characteristic to assess at this fundamental level of our information culture framework. Here, you should attempt to find out whether or not people are likely to be inclined to share information with their colleagues, and whether those colleagues will be limited to only those working in the same team or whether they will include those working in other departments.

The deciding factor here is likely to be related to national cultural characteristics. The tables provided in Chapter 2 relating to Hofstede's dimensions indicate that a view of sharing information as an attribute of organisational success versus a view of withholding information as an attribute of organisational success are characteristics relating to the individualist/collectivist dimension. In addition, the characteristic of openness with information is associated with countries that ranked low on the power distance dimension, whereas high power distance is associated with information constrained by hierarchy.

The key questions to be asked therefore are:

- Where is the organisation situated?

- Where are employees situated?

- What ranking does this/these place(s) have on the individualist/collectivist dimension?

- What ranking does this/these place(s) have on the power distance dimension?

Dimension rankings can easily be ascertained by using the online tool available at Geert Hofstede Cultural Dimensions Resources *http://www.geert-hofstede.com/geert_hofstede_resources.shtml.*

If your research reveals that either the whole or part of the organisation and its employees are based in a country which scores highly on the collectivist dimension and/or the power distance dimension, then be prepared to factor a reluctance to share information widely into the overall design of your information management system. A high score on the collectivist dimension, though, will probably indicate readiness to share information with colleagues in the same team, but a resistance to sharing with those outside this workgroup.

Another factor that will influence willingness to share information, which is not related to national cultural characteristics, relates to the function and purpose of the organisation, and the sector that it is operating in. Security requirements and competitiveness will both be factors that will inhibit willingness to share information with colleagues. So further questions could be:

- Are security classifications applied to routine operational activities?

- Do employee reward systems encourage individual rather than team approaches to activities?

An affirmative answer to either of these questions will certainly indicate that sharing information with colleagues is not likely to be encouraged, or even be the right thing to do. If there are security reasons why information should be restricted rather than shared then it is imperative that information management systems support these considerations. If reward systems promote hoarding rather than sharing information, then it would be worth checking to see that this is deliberate rather than an inadvertent consequence. For instance, if there are any aspirations voiced as to becoming a learning organisation, then it would be good to point out the inhibitory effect of the performance management systems that are in place. This feature is unique in terms of level one characteristics, as it could be easily influenced or changed if desired by the organisation.

Trust in information. This is the first of two factors in the assessment framework relating to trust, the other being at level three. At level one, this factor considers which are likely to be the most trusted primary sources for information, for example, individuals or text resources. The degree of trust will be evidenced by preference, i.e. which sources of information are preferred. Again, national cultural characteristics are likely to be significant. The tables in Chapter 2 indicate that two characteristics associated with differences on the individualist/ collectivist dimension are relevant here. The first characteristic relates to preferences for high context rather than low context information. This influences whether communication takes place based primarily on the context of the information, or on the explicit content. So if the preference is high context, images may communicate information adequately. If the preference is for low context, then words will definitely be needed. The second characteristic relates to preferences for relying more on one's social network as a source of information rather than relying on published sources.

So, the key questions to assess which information will be trusted and therefore used are:

- Where is the organisation situated?

- Where are employees situated?

- What ranking does this/these place(s) have on the individualist/collectivist dimension?

Dimension rankings can easily be ascertained by using the online tool available at Geert Hofstede Cultural Dimensions Resources *http://www.geert-hofstede.com/geert_hofstede_ resources.shtml.*

If the organisation and the majority of its employees are based in locations which score highly on the collectivist end of this dimension, there are likely to be preferences for non-textual information and perhaps less use of published (whether online or in traditional print format) resources for initial fact finding. However, I do not think that this factor can be solely interpreted based on analysis of a single cultural dimension. Further investigation as to the extent to which people are willing to trust their colleagues as opposed to rely on official written sources could be carried out. In this case, survey questions could be developed to find out employee preferences. For instance,

- If you need to find out what the requirements are to protect personal information in this organisation, what would be your first course of action:
  - Ask your manager?
  - Ask your colleague?
  - Check organisational policies on the intranet?

Consistent preferences for written sources such as the policy documents will indicate a high trust in textual information. Preferences for asking people will certainly emphasise the importance of training, and making sure that individuals are aware and up-to-date with the content of policy.

Language requirements. The languages that the organisation uses and needs to communicate with are fundamental features of its information culture and should be obvious. There may be constraints associated with particular character sets used and also the need for multilingual versions of information. This is a very straightforward factor to assess, but omitting to take this into consideration may result in unforeseen consequences when managing digital information. Key questions are:

- Is there a need to publish/disseminate/use information in more than one language?
- Do languages used have non-Roman characters?
- Do languages used have diacritical marks such as accents?

If the answer to any of these questions is yes, then make sure this is kept in mind when considering any strategies for the rendering of digital documents.

Regional technological infrastructure. This is the last of the level one characteristics and is a very practical feature that must be taken into account. It is particularly important, for instance, when considering guidance and advice developed in another region, which may quite simply be not applicable given local constraints. The technological infrastructure in place externally will be a profound influencing factor on the dimensions of the information culture within an organisation. It will affect which tools are used to manage information, the ways in which employees work, including the extent to which they are constrained by the physical boundary of the organisation. Determining the capabilities of the technological infrastructure which supports organisational systems will be relatively straightforward, as this information should be available from published resources. The Economist Intelligence Unit, for example, provides an annual ranking of e-readiness for over sixty countries (Economist Intelligence Unit, 2009).

Level two

The second level of the information culture assessment framework addresses employees' skills, knowledge and experience related to information management, which can be acquired and/or extended in the workplace. This should be the level that you target most attention to as this is where you can really make a big difference! The two categories to focus on are:

- Information-related competencies, including information and computer literacy. Do staff know how to evaluate the authority of information resources? Are staff aware of the need to assign appropriate metadata to documents they create? Are staff aware of the risks involved in using USB keys for data storage? And so on.

- Awareness of environmental (societal and organisational) requirements relating to information. Are staff aware of the legislative requirements to manage information in certain ways, for example to protect personal information? Are staff familiar with the requirements of relevant organisational policy?

Sometimes the focus of any training delivered by information management staff is solely on this last factor, the policy that has been developed in-house. This is not at all surprising as probably the information management team has spent many hours in crafting the required policy, developing associated procedures, and getting management approval for the whole package. But concentrating solely on raising awareness of, say, organisational records management requirements, will guarantee only partial success in accomplishing your overall goals of promoting effective information management. This is because staff simply may not have the contextual awareness necessary to understand why the policy is in place, and/or the skills necessary in order to conform to the policy. If either of these components is missing, then training objectives will not be realised.

The information that you have gathered to provide your level one assessment will probably have given you some insight into your organisation's employees' information-related competencies, and perhaps their awareness of information management requirements as well. So you may already have a good idea of which areas need to be addressed by training. However, particularly if you are responsible for information management in a large and dispersed organisation, more rigorous identification of training needs may need to be carried out. Requirements for information and computer literacy will vary according to individual responsibilities and the systems that are in use. Particular issues may range from information retrieval to managing information overload, as well as proficiency in using specific software packages. Target each level of your organisation, and try to get an overview of information management related training needs by asking staff about problems they experience in working with information. The method you use to ask staff will depend on the size and complexity of your organisation, and the information tools already available. So you may consider developing a short online survey for staff to complete, or perhaps just wander around and chat to some key people.

Determining awareness of societal and organisational requirements for managing information will be a straightforward process. The first step will be to identify all external requirements relating to information management, and then to see whether relevant organisational policies exist. The next stage will be to analyse the extent to which the content of the policy reflects the intent of the external requirement. (At this stage of course there may be remedial work required to upgrade the policy so that it does accurately reflect any external requirements.) The final step will be to find out whether individuals are aware of appropriate policies. This can be done by asking staff, or if policies are online it may be possible to view data relating to their usage. Although in this case, beware of the level one 'trust in information' characteristic which may skew your findings.

Assessment of people's knowledge and understanding of requirements to manage information, in conjunction with your observations and any information gathered for the analysis at level one, will provide you with a solid basis to identify learning objectives for your training programme. Once the learning objectives are clearly formulated the content will emerge. For example, if you have found out that staff are unaware of the reasons why a shared document repository should be used to save their work, then a learning objective could be 'Ensure staff are familiar with options for saving documents'. Content can then be developed which will emphasise the advantages and/or disadvantages of each option.

Almost as important as identifying training needs is deciding how the training should be delivered. Options are many and varied – here are a few of the decisions that will need to be made. Should training be delivered on an individual or group basis? If group, how should the groups be made up – by functional area or representing a range of different functions? Should groups be segregated by level of employee, or should they be cross-sectional in terms of organisational hierarchy? Will face to face contact be needed, or should online resources be developed? What types of supporting materials should be developed? Should external trainers be used, or will existing information management staff be sufficient?

It is important that your decision making here is based on the findings from your level one analysis. In other words, cultural characteristics play a critical role, in particular rankings on the power distance and individualist/collectivist dimensions.

If the employees of an organisation were raised and work in a country with a ranking at the collectivist end of the individualist/collectivist dimension (for example, China and South East Asian countries), then training is more likely to be effective if it is delivered on a group basis. The composition of the groups should reflect work units rather than be assembled from across the organisation. Also there is likely to be a preference for high context communication. This suggests that diagrams and images will be very effective as a means of communicating relevant training messages, and that these should be used in any supporting resources that are developed.

In contrast, for those employees who grew up and are working in a country with an extreme individualist ranking (Australia and the United States, for example), training focused at the individual level is more likely to be effective. In these countries the preference is likely to be for low context communication, so consideration should be given to providing explicit text-based resources for use as supporting references.

Rankings on the power distance dimension will influence whether training should be delivered to a cross-section of the organisational hierarchy or not. If the setting is one where there is a high score on the power distance dimension, i.e. status is accorded a high importance, then trying to deliver training to a group of participants representing all ranks will probably be doomed to failure. Those at the lower end would certainly not want to risk offending the boss and so would maintain a very low profile. Managers, on the other hand, would be wary of losing face and so would likely to be equally reluctant to fully participate. In this case it would also be wise to consider using a source of expertise for training which would be considered neutral – that is, not aligned to one particular organisational group.

The final decisions on these points and eventual design of your training programme will, of course, be constrained by the resources you have available (what funding is available, whether information management staff have the necessary expertise to develop and deliver training, and so on). But establishing first of all what likely cultural preferences there are will provide you with a firm foundation for a successful training programme to address the features represented at level two of the information culture framework. The final point to remember is that training should not be regarded as a one-off activity. Follow-up training needs should be considered, and new staff coming into the organisation should be identified and trained as soon as possible.

Level three

The uppermost level of the framework provides further data for the assessment of the information culture. The two features to be considered here are information governance and trust in organisational information systems.

Information governance. The information governance model that is in place will be reflected in the degree of coherence of the overall information architecture. A typology of information states developed by Thomas Davenport and colleagues (Davenport et al., 1992) provides an easy to apply template based on features that are very familiar to most of us. These authors identified five distinct models, which they depict as political states:

- *Information federalism.* This approach to information management is based on negotiation and consensus on the organisation's key information elements and reporting structures.

- *Information feudalism.* Here, individual business units manage their own information, define their own needs and report only limited information to the overall organisation.

- *Information monarchy.* In a monarchy, information categories and reporting structures are defined by the leaders of the organisation, who may or may not share information after collecting it.

- *Information anarchy.* As the name suggests, there is an absence of any overall information management policy, and individuals obtain and manage their own information.

- *Technocratic utopia.* This approach to information management is characterised by an emphasis on information engineering and technological solutions, particularly focusing on new and emerging technologies. (Davenport et al., 1992: 56)

In my experience, where information anarchy is the norm and this has been recognised as a problem, the solution that is proposed is often the technocratic utopia, the magic bullet which will bring everything under control. The reality, of course, will be quite different; if all information management problems could be addressed by the implementation of a technological system then our professional skills and expertise would not be needed. Which is most definitely not the case!

In order to determine which model typifies your organisation, try to find out the extent to which information systems interconnect. So the key questions will be:

- What functions does the organisation carry out?

- What information systems support those functions?

- Do the information systems use data that is common to all systems?

- Are single or multiple log-ons required to access these systems by individuals who need to use their information to carry out their work?

If you find that there is a pattern of multiple systems that do not interconnect, then beware of attempts to develop a new system to fix isolated problem areas. Find out what plans there are to address this area, and marshal your arguments against the deceptive lure of a technological utopia!

Trust in organisational systems. The final area that must be assessed in order to understand your organisation's information culture is to find out the extent to which employees trust existing in-house information management systems. This is critical – no matter how robust your systems are, if employees do not trust those systems, those employees will not use them. The result being, of course, that a large proportion of your efforts to establish comprehensive and effective information management efforts will have been in vain.

The consequences of lack of trust were vividly demonstrated to me when I carried out the case study of the Australian university. This university had a records management unit, which had been in existence for fourteen years. It was well resourced, in that it had five members of staff, all with professional qualifications in either records or archives. A filing system and retention schedule had been devised, and the scope of the records unit was enterprise wide, i.e. not limited to one department or function. So in terms of the framework level one factor, respect for information as evidence, there were plenty of signs to suggest that information as evidence was respected and valued by the organisation.

However, when I interviewed staff outside the records unit, I found that there was a marked tendency for people to keep their own files rather than add them to the central system. One manager described the situation in her area as an ongoing battle to get anyone to add records to the central filing system. The reason for this was a perception that files were destroyed before they should have been. Whether this was fact or fiction was immaterial, the point being that the filing system was perceived as being a place that could not be trusted to store the records needed for as long as they were required for operational purposes. It did not appear that this was a feature that could be addressed by modification of the retention and disposal schedule, which should provide the ultimate authority as to how long information needs to be kept. It was a case, quite simply, of lack of trust.

The lack of trust did indeed sabotage the effectiveness of the system. It was not just a question of not using files, but of withholding key documents. For instance, records relating to the negotiation and establishment of contracts and agreements might be filed, but the original signed copy of the agreement was kept 'safely' by the individual responsible for that area of work. This raises all sorts of problems relating to the proper storage and protection of the record, as the records unit had procedures in place to ensure appropriate security. A more disturbing aspect, though, is the risk that decisions would be made based on incomplete evidence. In the case of the contract, it would be relatively straightforward to spot the absence of the crucial record. But if the missing component was not so obvious, say in the case of a more unstructured correspondence file, then users of the file would be unaware that the information was incomplete.

Lack of trust can also be very detrimental to library operations. As with the records management system, signs of lack of trust in this setting can be witnessed as contributing factors to a desire to keep resources in the staff member's own working area, rather than in a central library; they will also be manifest in a lack of engagement with library services, the unfortunately familiar scenario where departments start building their own collections rather than using the organisation's library.

The key questions to be asked to gather data to assess the level of trust in organisational systems are quite straightforward:

- Are appropriate systems in place?
- Is information withheld from systems?
- Are there any significant barriers to use, such as location of a physical repository in a location remote from users, or insufficient access to technological systems?

If the answer to the first two questions is yes, and no to the third, the most likely cause of the problem is lack of trust. Once this has been identified then an ongoing programme to modify perceptions will have to be developed. Establishing trust is not easy, it will take ongoing effort and there will be a need to work hard on relationship building as well as continually demonstrating responsiveness to user needs.

Conclusions

This chapter has explored the concept of information culture, and provided a framework to use in order to assess it. Unlike information audits or surveys, the emphasis is not on what information is created, available and used, but rather on the ways in which people behave, and inherent values and attitudes which will impact on the way that information is managed. The framework distinguishes between factors which can be changed, and those that cannot, but including both emphasises the requirement for solutions tailored to the organisation's needs. The final chapter provides four different scenarios of information management projects to demonstrate how different strategies for implementation will have to be developed in order to take into account variation in organisational setting.

References

Davenport, T. H., R. G. Eccles & L. Prusak (1992) Information politics. *Sloan Management Review* (Fall), 53–65.

Economist Intelligence Unit (2009) *The 2007 e-readiness rankings* from *http://www.eiu.com/site_info.asp?info_name=eiu_2007_e_readiness_rankings*.

7

Scenarios

Abstract: This chapter presents four different scenarios, each relating to the implementation of a new information management initiative. The four scenarios are: establishing a special library service, developing a business case of a digital library, implementing an electronic document and records management system and establishing an in-house archival repository. Each scenario is considered in the context of four contrasting organisational types. For each setting, the main issues are identified and appropriate strategies to gain organisational acceptance are suggested.

Key words: special library service, digital library, electronic records management, EDRMS, archives.

Introduction

This chapter considers four information management activities, and the issues and challenges faced in their implementation in different organisational cultures. These activities are: establishing a special library service, developing a business case for a digital library, implementing an electronic document and records management system (EDRMS), and establishing an in-house archival repository. The four broad types of organisations (village market, family model, full bureaucracy and well-oiled machine) introduced in Chapter 2 are used to provide a consistent set of variable settings in which to review each activity. In the real world, of course, complexities relating to the different occupational cultures also present within organisations would also have to be taken into account. Before presenting the scenarios, the main features of the organisational types are summarised.

Organisation types

These four organisation types were first described by Dr Richard Mead, who categorised them as bureaucratic models (Mead, 2005: 181). 'Bureaucracy' is not used in a pejorative sense, but as a generic term encompassing all organisations that apply rules to govern the behaviour of their members. The type and extent of these rules (or policies) reflect the type of organisation. The Dutch anthropologist Geert Hofstede associated each bureaucratic model with correlations of national cultural rankings on the dimensions of power distance and uncertainty avoidance. The features of each model are described below, and indications given as to where in the world these organisation types are likely to be situated. As with all discussions of national culture, it must be emphasised that identifying specific countries or regions should not be taken to mean that all organisations located there will be of the same type. However, it is more likely that a certain type will be represented, or may even predominate, in that location.

Marketplace bureaucracy or village market model

This bureaucratic model is likely to be found in countries where there is a correlation between a low ranking on the power distance dimension together with a low need to avoid uncertainty about the future. So this organisation type is most likely in countries such as Britain, Australia and New Zealand. A characteristic feature is that more importance is likely to be accorded to relationships between people, than to rules and regulations (Mead, 1990: 26) thus influence may be negotiated across departmental lines. Richard Mead describes the underlying philosophy as 'If you scratch my back, I'll scratch yours' (Mead, 2005: 181).

In Chapter 2 I identified the main features of organisational work that may impact on information management, based on Hofstede's analysis. Those characteristics for the marketplace bureaucracy are as follows:

- decentralised decision structures;
- flat organisational structure;
- small proportion of supervisory personnel;
- ideal boss who is a resourceful democrat, sees self as practical, orderly, relying on support;
- managers relying on personal experience and on subordinates;
- subordinates who expect to be consulted;
- a view of consultative leadership as leading to satisfaction, performance and productivity;
- innovations that need good champions;
- openness with information, also to non-superiors;
- short average duration of employment;
- scepticism towards technological solutions;
- innovators who feel independent of rules;
- renegade championing;
- top managers involved in strategy;
- power of superiors depending on position and relationships;

- tolerance for ambiguity in structures and procedures;
- bias towards transformational leader role;
- innovations welcomed but not necessarily taken seriously;
- employees who will have to learn and manage precision and punctuality;
- relationship orientation;
- belief in generalists and common sense.

Full bureaucracy or pyramid model

At the opposite extreme to the marketplace bureaucracy is the full bureaucracy. This organisational model is typical in countries which have a high ranking on the power distance dimension, with a similarly high ranking in terms of the need to avoid uncertainty about the future. Full bureaucracies are most likely to be found in Latin, Mediterranean and Islamic countries, as well as Japan and some other Asian countries. Richard Mead describes this organisation type as most reflective of the Weberian ideal (Mead, 2005: 182) and is closest to our popular conception of a bureaucracy, with all the accompanying negative connotations that entails. The key features of work which may be relevant to any consideration of information management in these organisation types were identified in Chapter 2, and are as follows:

- centralised decision structures;
- hierarchical organisation structure;
- large proportion of supervisory personnel;
- ideal boss who is well-meaning autocrat, regards self as benevolent decision maker;
- managers relying on formal rules;

- subordinates who expect to be told;
- a view of authoritative leadership and close supervision as leading to satisfaction, performance and productivity;
- innovations that need good support from hierarchy;
- information constrained by hierarchy;
- long average duration of employment;
- bias towards technological solutions;
- innovators who feel constrained by rules;
- rational championing;
- top managers involved in operations;
- power of superiors depending on control of uncertainties;
- highly formalised management;
- bias towards hierarchical control role;
- innovations resisted but if accepted applied consistently;
- employees to whom precision and punctuality come naturally;
- task orientation;
- belief in specialists and expertise.

Personnel bureaucracy or family model

The third bureaucratic model is one that is mostly likely to be found in China, India, Hong Kong, Singapore, West Africa – all places that have a high ranking in terms of power distance, coupled with a low need to avoid uncertainty about the future. This organisation type is characterised by having a strong leader, whose authority is associated with them as an individual, which is not necessarily the same as authority associated with a rank or position. Richard Mead suggests that promotion will be more likely for in-group or family members, and difficult if not impossible for outsiders. Mead provides an insider's view of the impact of these cultural traditions, quoting an Indian manager:

> Lack of knowledge of one's role and that of others one comes into contact with is one of the foremost causes of employee and organizational ineffectiveness ... Relationships often fail due to misunderstandings and lack of role clarity, as can be seen in the example of the old employee trying to play the role of adviser to a new employee who misinterprets this as being 'bossed' by one who has no business to do so! (Mead, 2005: 183)

The implications of this for any knowledge transfer projects are immense. The other key features of work which may be relevant to any consideration of information management in these organisation types were identified in Chapter 2, and are as follows:

- centralised decision structures;
- hierarchical organisation structure;
- large proportion of supervisory personnel;
- ideal boss who is well-meaning autocrat, regards self as benevolent decision maker;
- managers relying on formal rules;
- subordinates who expect to be told;
- a view of authoritative leadership and close supervision as leading to satisfaction, performance and productivity;
- innovations that need good support from hierarchy;
- information constrained by hierarchy;
- short average duration of employment;
- scepticism towards technological solutions;

- innovators who feel independent of rules;
- renegade championing;
- top managers involved in strategy;
- power of superiors depending on position and relationships;
- tolerance for ambiguity in structures and procedures;
- bias towards transformational leader role;
- innovations welcomed but not necessarily taken seriously;
- employees who will have to learn and manage precision and punctuality;
- relationship orientation;
- belief in generalists and common sense.

Workflow bureaucracy or well-oiled machine

The final organisation type is most likely to be found in the German-speaking countries of Germany, Switzerland and Austria, where national culture is characterised by a low ranking on the power distance dimension, coupled with a high need to avoid uncertainty about the future. In these organisations, greater emphasis is placed on regulating activities rather than negotiating relationships. Richard Mead singles out a societal feature to differentiate the impact of this organisational type: the ease with which German trade unions, management and government appear to cooperate in order to, for instance, implement new technologies (Mead, 2005: 183).

The characteristics relating to the workflow bureaucracy identified in Chapter 2 are as follows:

- decentralised decision structures;
- flat organisational structure;
- small proportion of supervisory personnel;

- ideal boss who is a resourceful democrat, see self as practical, orderly, relying on support;
- managers relying on personal experience and on subordinates;
- subordinates who expect to be consulted;
- a view of consultative leadership as leading to satisfaction, performance and productivity;
- innovations that need good champions;
- openness with information, also to non-superiors;
- long average duration of employment;
- bias towards technological solutions;
- innovators who feel constrained by rules;
- rational championing;
- top managers involved in operations;
- power of superiors depending on control of uncertainties;
- highly formalised management;
- bias towards hierarchical control role;
- innovations resisted but if accepted applied consistently;
- employees to whom precision and punctuality come naturally;
- task orientation;
- belief in specialists and expertise.

Scenario one: establishing a special library service

In this scenario the situation is one where there is a need for a library service in order to provide specialist information to support the work undertaken by professional staff within the organisation. The organisation itself could be either in the private sector (for example, a law firm or pharmaceutical company) or public (a government-funded research institute, for instance).

Referring back to our information culture assessment framework described in Chapter 6, the key factor to be addressed is respect for information as knowledge. In other words, the extent to which there is within the organisation recognition and awareness of the need to manage certain information for the purpose of increasing knowledge and awareness.

The other factors that are likely to be highly influential in this particular scenario are considerations relating to occupational culture. Which professions are represented within the organisation, who would be the primary users of the library service are key questions to be answered.

Marketplace bureaucracy or village market model

In the marketplace bureaucracy or village market organisational type, in order to establish a library service a good first step would be to spend time consulting with the specialists who will be the main users. The aim of the consultation would be to find out how their information needs are currently met, and what strategies they perceive as being of assistance. Ascertain how people currently work, and then use this as a basis to design the library service. Beware of developing a proposal that could be perceived by the target group as being detrimental to their needs. For instance, in this organisation type characterised by a flat and possibly ambiguous structure, the acquisition of information resources may be ad hoc and purchases made on an individual basis. So if staff are used to regarding their information resources as individually owned, any proposal for centralisation and rationalisation may be regarded as a barrier to efficient and effective working.

It will be essential to demonstrate cost-effectiveness, but the emphasis should be on how to achieve this without disturbing patterns of working that are perceived by users as being optimum. Support from users will be essential for the successful implementation of a library service, so a good strategy will be to collect and/or develop narratives of specific instances where fast access to accurate information has made a difference to a situation which is germane to the work of the organisation.

In this organisational type it will be necessary to find a champion to fight for and represent this initiative. Try to identify someone who is genuinely enthusiastic and realises the value of library service. This is likely to be someone who is part of the target user group, but care should be taken to make sure they represent all the occupational cultures involved, and not just their own 'tribe'. Consideration should be given to establishing a management committee, in order to involve representation from each specialist user community. It will also be important to undertake regular service evaluation, and to provide responsive feedback to users.

Full bureaucracy or pyramid model

In this organisation type, the approach to establishing a special library service would be very different to its polar opposite organisation described above. Instead of focusing on the users and mobilising their support, primary attention should be targeted at managing upwards. In other words, convincing the next layer above in the organisational hierarchy of the importance and need for a library service, and providing support to enable that supervisory layer to convince their managers, and so on. Attempting to garner support without proceeding systematically upwards through a chain of command is not likely to be successful.

Services should still of course be designed and developed to suit user needs. However, when identifying which users to target for interview, the most senior individuals should be approached. These will be the people with the most influence within the organisation, so it will be critical to enlist their support.

All library policies and procedures should be clearly and systematically documented, and authorised by senior management. It will be particularly important to demonstrate clear pathways for decision making, for instance the purchase of resources. The mission of the library should emphasise its value in supporting the work of specialists. A particularly challenging feature, which may appear to be at odds with the fundamental role of libraries in facilitating the freedom of information, is consideration of whether information needs to be restricted to particular hierarchical levels rather than be made openly available to all staff within the organisation. If this can be done without compromising the role of the library then it should be seriously considered.

Personnel bureaucracy or family model

In this model, approval and authorisation must be gained from the strong leader who will be found in this organisation type. If the library is to provide services to all departments in the organisation it will probably be essential to ensure that structurally the library reports directly to the leader. If this is not the case, then there is a serious risk that the library would be seen as aligned to one particular area and so not relevant to others.

Once again, consideration should be given to whether or not information should be restricted according to hierarchical levels, rather than being made freely available across the organisation. In this setting, it could be the case that restrictions are implemented based on physical access to the library space, in other words, only designated employees would be permitted to enter the library.

The key characteristic of belief in generalists and common sense rather than specialists and expertise does not imply that organisations of this type would have a particularly receptive environment for library services. Although this is also true of the marketplace bureaucracy, in that setting an appropriate strategy to offset this was to enlist the support of those users. The personnel bureaucracy model does not present similar opportunities. There is no way around the need for buy in and support by the organisation's leader. If that is not forthcoming then the initiative will simply not succeed. So, analysis of the leader's information needs, and identification of concerns relating to unauthorised access to information must be very carefully carried out. Then attempts must be made to develop and tailor services for that individual, and hopefully by actual demonstration of benefits support will be forthcoming.

Workflow bureaucracy or well-oiled machine

In this organisation type, negotiation and involvement of all target user groups in the design and delivery of library services will be essential. In contrast to the personnel bureaucracy, specialists and expertise are likely to be highly regarded in these organisations, which would certainly seem to be a positive and receptive environment for the development of a library service.

As in the case of the full bureaucracy, clearly documented policies and procedures will be essential, together with authorisation of senior management. Technological solutions are likely to be favoured. As information technology architecture is likely to be holistically designed rather than characterised by ad hoc growth, a good approach would be to investigate how to leverage the use of existing systems to deploy library services.

Scenario two: developing a business case for a digital library

In this scenario the assumption is that the organisation has an established, traditional library service but that a need has been perceived to develop a digital library. As a further twist we will assume that the person who has recognised the need is not at the top of the library's management hierarchy; in other words, someone who cannot rely on any innate power or authority to influence the decision makers. The key challenge here is to present a case for change from an established service delivery model to one utilising new and emerging technologies.

As in the preceding scenario, a key consideration will be the extent to which the organisation respects information as knowledge, or the level of awareness of the need to manage information for the purpose of increasing knowledge and awareness. Unlike the previous scenario, though, this is demonstrated to a certain extent because there is already a library service in existence. This digital library scenario has been selected because it will highlight issues relating to less senior information management professionals and to the implementation of emerging technologies.

Marketplace bureaucracy or village market model

In this organisation type, convincing professional library colleagues of the need for a digital library will be as essential as gaining user input into the development of a business case. The first step, therefore, will be to identify who the stakeholders are, and what roles have to be considered. Representatives from all levels of the organisation should be involved in consultation; this must not be restricted simply to upper levels of management.

It will be necessary to cultivate a champion for this project who will be able to influence decision making at key resource allocation meetings. However, it will not necessarily be a disadvantage for the initiative to originate from a lower level in the organisation's management structure, provided widespread support can be demonstrated.

Any written documentation required must include a standalone executive summary which encapsulates all the key points, including recommendations and funding implications. Although supporting details will undoubtedly be required and expected, there is no guarantee that the decision makers will read the detail, so a comprehensive, easily digestible précis is essential. Similarly, any presentations should be jargon free; decision makers are unlikely to be convinced or impressed by the use of technical language.

One feature to be wary of in this environment is the juxtaposition of 'a scepticism towards technological solutions', and 'innovations welcomed but not necessarily taken seriously'. This implies that there may be apparent interest in a new initiative such as developing a digital library, but that this may only be at a very superficial level because of novelty value rather than any intrinsic recognition of appropriateness. So whereas it may be relatively easy to capture initial interest in the project, capitalising on that is likely to be more difficult and will require sustained effort.

Full bureaucracy or pyramid model

At the opposite extreme in terms of organisation types, in this environment a business case could only be developed if it had the full support of the initiator's manager. An initiative such as this which challenges the existing order of things would not be welcomed, and the innovator would be at quite a disadvantage without the power and prestige that a senior role brings. Whether or not colleagues, particularly subordinates, supported the idea would have little impact on its progress. Authorisation would have to be obtained systematically through each level upwards in the chain of command. The main stumbling block is likely to be right at the start, that is, getting people to accept that the idea has merit and give permission to proceed to gather data to support a case.

Likely cultural preferences could be taken into account in the digital library functionality outlined in the business case. This organisation type is likely to have a bias towards technological solutions, so much should be made of efficiency gains to be realised from developing a digital library in contrast to existing physical systems. A preference for information to be constrained by hierarchy suggests that social networking features would not be highly regarded enhancements. Platforms to share information and engage in discussion may not be seen as appropriate or desirable in this organisational context.

Full documentation would have to be prepared to justify the business case, with benefits and costs itemised. The approval process is likely to be lengthy, but at least the appropriate pathway for authorisation would be clear and unambiguous.

Personnel bureaucracy or family model

As with the traditional library service scenario, the essential step would be to gain approval to proceed from the organisation's leader. Convincing this person of the value and benefits to be gained from a digital library is critical to success – without this person's support the initiative will fail. If the project proceeds beyond the business case stage it will be essential, if it is to be implemented organisation wide, that it is not aligned with any particular department.

As with the previous organisation type, it will be necessary for the initiator of the idea to proceed upwards through their management hierarchy, rather than approaching the leader directly. It will not be necessary to enlist support from subordinates.

In this environment, innovations may have novelty value, which will be of key assistance in getting that initial hearing. The challenge, of course, will be to capitalise on that initial interest and demonstrate the likely benefits to the organisation of implementing a digital library.

Thorough documentation will be required, but it is likely to be important for this to be presented in non-technical language. Professional jargon will not be appreciated. It is also likely that good use of visual imagery will be required. Organisations of this type are situated in regions which have a high ranking in terms of collectivism, which has been associated with preferences for high context communication (see Chapter 2). So using graphs to illustrate efficiencies and benefits will be very appropriate.

As with the full bureaucracy, a characteristic of the personnel bureaucracy is a view of restricting information according to hierarchy as necessary. The functionality presented in the business case should therefore reflect this view and emphasise abilities to collaborate within workgroups or teams rather than organisation wide.

Workflow bureaucracy or well-oiled machine

Involvement of all stakeholders in the development of the business case in this organisation type will be essential. Colleagues, subordinates, managers and users should all be consulted and their opinions incorporated into the justification. The documentation itself should reflect and detail the consultative process.

The business case should also overtly draw on external resources, for example using and citing similar initiatives to support the arguments made. It will really strengthen the business case if a solid, evidence base can be demonstrated and show that the idea is founded on other successful endeavours in a similar organisational setting. National and international standards should be referred to where possible, as these are likely to be trusted by management.

The favourable components in this environment are that there is likely to be a bias towards technological solutions, and furthermore that openness with information is encouraged. Incorporating a digital library into existing information technology infrastructure is likely to be achievable, and so this should be capitalised on. Elucidating how digital library usage can enhance existing workflows and including this detail in a business case is likely to be a winning strategy. Using specialist, technical language in a business case is likely to garner respect from decision makers rather than the reverse.

Scenario three: implementing an electronic document and records management system (EDRMS)

This scenario is one which has caused many problems in both private and public sector organisations in western developed economies. The aim of EDRMS systems is to manage digital records; in other words to provide the functionality of physical filing systems for paper records in technological form. Unfortunately, however, that involves quite substantial change to the way that people work, as implicit in the implementation of these systems is the expectation that everyone will carry out records management tasks. These may well be minimal, such as filing documents in the records system by dragging and dropping, but even such small tasks require buy-in and cooperation from users.

Consequently this is a setting which really highlights differences in terms of the value that is accorded to information as evidence, that is the recognition and awareness of the need to manage certain information for the purposes of accountability. Also playing a key role in this scenario is the regulatory environment; that is, what legislative requirements there are for the management of records, and the attitudes of staff towards compliance. In the paper environment, responsibility for keeping records was likely to have been firmly delegated to administrative support staff, but that situation no longer prevails.

Marketplace bureaucracy or village market model

This organisation type appears to be particularly unsuited for the implementation of an EDRMS, which is unfortunate to say the least given that the EDRMS is currently the predominant solution for the management of digital records. Key problematic characteristics include managers relying on personal experience, as this implies that recordkeeping will not be viewed as essential. The tolerance for ambiguity in structures and procedures suggests that the formality associated with recordkeeping may be regarded as excessive and unnecessary. The characteristic of employees needing to learn and manage precision and punctuality again conveys the ambiguity and lack of clarity associated with this organisational type.

Gaining the co-operation and support of users will be essential for successful implementation. The additional work practices (however minor) associated with EDRMS implementation are likely to be regarded as impositions so it is essential that this aspect is explicitly addressed rather than ignored. To do this successfully, appropriate training programmes must be implemented. 'Appropriate' means designing according to user needs and preferences. So training is likely to consist of a number of components including small group sessions and online tutorials for solo study, as well as being supplemented by help desk and/or floor-walking backup. Neglecting users, or attempting to economise on efforts in this regard will inevitably lead to the aims of the system being undermined. For an EDRMS to be successful, usage has to be consistent and routine otherwise the records that are being managed will not reflect the entirety of the organisation's memory.

Use of the EDRMS may appear to impose a formality of working which can seem at odds with the characteristic informal, relationship-based working environment. So it is essential that the records management team should recognise this, and search for ways to compensate for it. One broad strategy should be to position themselves as an integral part of the organisation, to work on relationship building rather than take literally the back room designation so often applied. A champion will definitely be required, someone at a senior level who can be relied on to show good practice. In this scenario representation by senior management is extremely important, as filing can still be regarded as the province of the lowly paid and most junior employees.

A final useful strategy should be the proactive documentation of instances where disasters have occurred as a result of poor recordkeeping. Associating records management with risk management can be an important way of emphasising the importance of utilising EDRMS for senior management.

Full bureaucracy or pyramid model

In this environment, which is characterised by the formality of processes, the implementation of an EDRMS presents a quite different set of issues and challenges. Unlike the market bureaucracy, if appropriate authorisation from management is forthcoming, imposing additional tasks on users should not present too many problems. Where problems do arise, however, is when there are concerns about widespread dissemination of information or unauthorised access to information both internally and externally.

Consequently perhaps the most important feature to be addressed will relate to security. Mapping functions and responsibilities within the organisation to information needs must be prioritised and, most importantly, decisions made should be authorised by appropriate levels within the chain of command. This feature should be highlighted when presenting any training seminars or workshops. In addition, ensuring that records are protected from unauthorised access from outside the organisation will assist in promoting confidence in the system.

Formalised management, bias towards hierarchical control role and preferences for technological solutions are all factors which should help provide a positive and receptive environment for EDRMS implementation. Add to that employees for whom precision and punctuality come naturally and a task orientation, then it is only fears relating to freedom of access that will need to be overcome.

Personnel bureaucracy or family model

Similar concerns are likely to be present in the personnel bureaucracy organisation type. Support from the strong leader will be essential, and the ideal would be to align the system and those responsible for its administration with this leadership role. If the EDRMS was managed by a section that was part of a particular functional area (for instance, student administration within a university) then there is a strong likelihood that it would be perceived as only serving that functional unit and not others.

The view of information as something which should be restricted rather than shared widely must be at the forefront when designing the configuration and implementation of the system. Personnel bureaucracy organisation types are typical of countries which rank highly on the collectivism dimension. So incorporating features which allow information sharing in workgroups while restricting access to 'outsiders' in other departments is likely to be a successful strategy. This feature can also be promoted in a slightly different way, that is to show that secretarial and administrative support staff will more easily be able to manage their superior's information.

Similarly, highlighting features that enable collaborative working within teams or workgroups is likely to assist with uptake. Training programmes are most likely to be successful if they are run on that workgroup basis. However, care should be taken not to include representatives from too diverse levels of the organisational hierarchy. Status is taken very seriously, and this could lead in subordinates not participating and senior personnel losing face. Given the likely preference for high context information, pictures and images rather than extensive text should be preferred for training materials.

Workflow bureaucracy or well-oiled machine

This organisation type appears to be the one most suited to EDRMS implementation. There is likely to be a bias towards technological solutions, coupled with a task orientation. Furthermore, the characteristic of openness with information suggest that concerns about unauthorised access within the organisation are not likely to present difficulties. Also, if there is recognition of the need for later, societal access to records then there is likely to be a pre-disposition to ensuring that records are created and managed appropriately as part of routine working requirements.

Problems associated with the other organisation types and the need to justify records management, and to restrict access to information, are not characteristic of the workflow bureaucracy. Although the EDRMS may necessitate different ways of working, the fundamental task of recordkeeping is more likely to be familiar and accepted in this environment. All legislative and standards-related requirements to recordkeeping should be made explicit, as these are likely to be respected and followed. Access restrictions will of course be necessary still, but these will reflect regulatory requirements such as privacy concerns. Once again, the motivation for restrictions must be made clear.

Scenario four: establishing an in-house archives repository

This scenario is quite possibly the most challenging one. Archives are poorly understood by the general public – unlike libraries, usage of archives is not something that can be relied on to have taken place in the course of education. Consequently the case to establish an in-house repository will have to be very carefully formulated in order to counteract likely pre-existing biases.

Records that are worth preserving for posterity are records that have been deemed to have archival value. As a rule of thumb, less than 10% of an organisation's records will fall into this category. In order to keep this scenario as simple as possible, it is assumed that the repository will be required for hard copy (mostly paper) records only. The ongoing preservation of digital records is complex, and omitted from consideration here because of the complications of the requirements for specialist expertise that would be introduced.

The permanent retention of analogue records is costly. A secure environment will be required, and control of temperature, humidity and light are essential as each of these factors can cause irreparable damage to materials. Archives cannot be stored in any old boxes or filing equipment that happens to be at hand, as these items are not likely to afford sufficient protection and may in themselves cause further damage. Consequently, containers such as acid-free boxes have to be purchased. Also, specialist expertise will be needed for the intellectual work associated with the management of archives such as arrangement and description. This cursory outline of basic requirements for a repository should indicate the not-trivial nature of this endeavour. Taking into consideration that these records are unlikely to have current operational value, it can be seen that establishing an in-house archival repository may not be a priority for organisations.

As with the EDRMS scenario, a key consideration will be the extent to which there is respect for information as evidence within the organisation. If this is absent or lacking, a much more difficult task is presented.

Marketplace bureaucracy or village market model

In the EDRMS scenario for this organisation type I argued that the need to create and maintain records is not likely to be regarded as being of an essential nature. Consequently it cannot be assumed that the regard for the value and importance of records will exist, let alone awareness of the need for permanent retention of some records with all the costs involved. Furthermore, this organisation type is characterised by periods of employment likely to be short. The implication of ongoing staff turnover is that there is unlikely to be regard for the need to maintain a history of the organisation.

If, however, an archives repository could be presented as enhancing the profile of the organisation then a positive case could be formulated. This is where careful analysis of the organisation's corporate culture, particularly its external image, will be useful. For instance, if traditional values or the long-standing expertise of craftsmen are invoked in advertising products, then the management of the organisation should be receptive to the idea of preserving its past. In this instance, using archival material in exhibitions will help demonstrate their value.

A less cynical view might be of an organisation that has a strong association with social justice such as welfare or political activism. Pride in the achievements of the organisation should be a strong motivator to tap into to gain support for the establishment of an archives.

Full bureaucracy or pyramid model

The highly formalised management and long average duration of employment in this organisational model may provide a positive setting for the establishment of an archival repository. The problem once again, though, is that there is likely to be an unwillingness to allow access to archived documents. Policies and procedures associated with the management of the archives would have to be prepared, and authorised by senior management. These policies should take into account concerns about access, and will have to demonstrate that appropriate measures will be taken to protect the archives from both environmental and human risks.

Personnel bureaucracy or family model

A key feature of this model is the existence of a strong leader, whose authority is associated with them as an individual, rather than with the rank and position. This provides a unique opportunity which can be capitalised upon. A focus of the archives could be on records and memorabilia associated with the individuals who have held that leadership role. Emphasising the commemorative possibilities associated with archives could very well be beneficial; organising displays of appropriate records will help make this point.

The notion of establishing an organisational genealogy may well fit with cultural preferences for vertical integration (see Chapter 2).

The concern that would have to be addressed is, as with the full bureaucracy, vulnerability of information to unauthorised access. The presence of a guardian or gatekeeper is likely to be essential.

Workflow bureaucracy or well-oiled machine

The likelihood of good recordkeeping practices applied to the management of current information suggests that this organisational type will be pre-disposed to the concept of archival records and the need to manage these appropriately. A high regard for the need for evidential records to demonstrate accountability for future generations provides the right philosophical underpinning for the establishment of an archives. In addition, recent history of state abuses of power in countries where this organisation type is likely to predominate emphasises the need for archival records to provide justice and enlightenment.

A high regard for openness with information suggests that this feature should be emphasised. In addition, any legal or regulatory requirements for archival records should be identified and emphasised as compliance is likely to be regarded as essential.

Conclusions

This chapter has attempted to demonstrate the sort of differences in approach which will be necessary in order to progress key information management initiatives in different organisational settings. Using the bureaucracy typology has enabled the application of the same set of variables to each initiative. In the real world, however, this would not provide the detailed cultural understanding that is fundamental for successful information management. The methodology outlined in the previous chapter provides the framework to proceed beyond stereotypical, broad-brush categorisations.

References

Mead, R. (1990) *Cross-cultural Management Communication*. New York: Wiley.

Mead, R. (2005) *International Management: Cross-cultural dimensions*, 3rd edn. Oxford: Blackwell.

Conclusion

For information managers, understanding and getting to grips with organisational culture is difficult but necessary. One of the key points to bear in mind, which has hopefully become clear throughout this book, is that there will be significant features which cannot be changed. These features could be linked to national or occupational cultures, or the structural environment which encompasses language, technological infrastructure and legislation. What is important, however, is to be able to distinguish and map these features, so that strategies can be developed which will take them into account. The alternative is that information managers will invest much time and energy into developing well-intentioned proposals or services that may be doomed to failure at the outset.

Awareness of the complexity of influences which contribute to shaping organisational culture is essential in our globalised world. Organisations conduct business beyond national boundaries; economic forces motivate the establishment of off-shore enterprises; and the boundaries of organisations are no longer likely to be fixed to one precise geographical location. International recognition of qualifications opens the doors for greater mobility of employees, so that the staff of an organisation may comprise a wide-ranging mixture of people with different values and attitudes towards information. Similarly, information managers also have greater opportunities for employment in unfamiliar environments. All of these situations call for greater acknowledgement of organisational culture and its influence on the way that information can be managed.

Focus on 'information culture' will help avoid getting caught in the terminology trap that besets the concept of organisational culture. The misconception of organisational culture as an entity that can be shaped and moulded as required is particularly prevalent in those parts of the world influenced by Anglo-American management theory. Trying to argue the case for a more nuanced understanding of organisational culture may well appear overly pedantic, so information managers are well advised to steer clear of all possible ambiguity and use the opportunities afforded by the concept of information culture.

The framework provided in this book is intended as a practical tool for the assessment of information culture, and therefore a basis for action. There is much more research and analysis necessary to test and refine the utility of this model, but it should be viewed as a starting point. Unless we collect data which can be used to inform decision making, the practice of information management in organisations will continue to be haphazard and uneven. Information managers need to demonstrate their awareness of the complexity of the organisations they work within, and thus ensure that they continue to be able to play a central and highly valued role. In today's challenging information environment, where every employee may have access to immense information resources from their desktop, information managers risk being regarded as unnecessary. The paradox is, of course, that information managers are even more essential than ever before, but our practice must be more attuned to our local operating environments. The sophistication necessary for this to happen can only come about by engaging with organisational, and therefore information, culture.

Index

Printed and bound by CPI Group (UK) Ltd, Croydon, CR0 4YY

13/05/2025

01869808-0001